THE

BANDITTI OF THE PRAIRIES

THE
BANDITTI OF THE PRAIRIES

A TALE

OF THE

MISSISSIPPI VALLEY

BY
EDWARD BONNEY

WILDSIDE PRESS

Published by Wildside Press LLC.
wildsidepress.com | bcmystery.com

THE
BANDITTI OF THE PRAIRIES

THE BANDITTI OF THE PRAIRIES.

A TALE OF THE MISSISSIPPI VALLEY.

CHAPTER. I.

THE valley of the Mississippi River from its earliest settlement has been more infested with reckless and blood-stained men, than any other part of the country, being more congenial to their habits and offering the greatest inducements to follow their nefarious and dangerous trade.

Situated as it is, of great commercial importance, and the river whose name it bears, together with its tributaries stretching four thousand miles north from the Gulf of Mexico, and draining all the country south and west of the great chain of Lakes, and between the Alleghany and Rocky Mountains, it has afforded them an unequalled chance to escape detection and pursuit, and thus wooed as it were, countless villains and blood-stained, law-doomed ones to screen themselves in its bosom.

Organized bands, trampling upon right, and defying all law human or divine, have so annoyed the peaceful and quiet citizens of this great valley, that in the absence of a sufficient judicial power the aid of "Judge Lynch" has been but too frequently called in, and a neighboring tree proved a gallows and "a short shrift and strong cord" been the doom of those who have ever plead vainly for mercy at his bar.

But this mode of summary punishment only served to drive those really guilty from one section of the country to another, changing for a time their plan of action and operations, without, in the least, reforming or exterminating them, while in many instances the innocent were made to atone for the crime of the guilty.

It would be useless to attempt to enumerate the thousand robberies and scores of murders committed from time to time by the organized and lawless Banditti, and our task shall be simply and plainly to detail the particulars of a few of the many committed by that portion of the gang infesting the country bordering on the Upper Mississippi. To track them plainly and fearlessly—to visit them in their most secret hiding places, and expose their most hidden plans, is the purpose of this narrative. This will include, fully, the particulars of the murder of Miller and Liecy in Lee County, Iowa, also that of Col. George Davenport at Rock Island, in the State of Illinois; also the pursuit, capture, arrest, trial, conviction and execution of Stephen and William Hodges, John and Aaron Long, and Glanvill Young: the pursuit, arrest, and escape of Wm. Fox and Robert Birch, and conviction of John Baxter, with the names and places of residence of a large number of the gang who are yet at large and unsuspected, with their mode of operations in their daring robberies and murders.

Such is the tale we have undertaken, and we enter upon it fearlessly, in the firm belief that we shall be sustained and repaid for the time and money it has cost to procure the many facts here set down. At once, then, we begin.

In the fall and winter of 1844, a large number of robberies and murders of the most daring and blood-thirsty kind, were committed, and yet so perfect was the organization of the perpetrators that all efforts to bring them to justice, proved abortive. So great indeed was the terror that they had inspired, that the good, quiet and orderly citizens, before retiring to rest at night, made all preparations for resistance that were in their power, and armed to the teeth, with doors and windows securely barred and bolted, laid down in fear and trembling to wish for the return of morning again.

Among the robberies committed was that of a stage belonging to Frink, Walker & Co., near Rockford, Illinois. A plan had long been on foot to rob the Dixon Land Office, and this was the end to be accomplished by the robbery of the stage. It was well known to many that a large amount of money, received from the sales of the public land, was deposited there and was about to be removed. One of the gang, in order to ascertain the particulars and the precise time of its removal, took occasion to ask the Receiver " when he intended to go to Chicago;" that being the place where the deposit was to be made. The Receiver, however, being upon his guard, and a prudent man, set the time one week later than he intended to start, and thereby baffled the preconcerted schemes of the robbers.

At the time designated for making the deposit, the stage coach was intercepted, and a trunk taken which was supposed to contain the land office money. Nothing, however, of value was found in it, with the exception of some rich clothing. Great exertions were made to ascertain who were guilty, but without avail, and the caution of the Receiver was the safeguard.

Some time in the winter of 1844 or early in 1845, it was rumored that a Mr. Mulford in Ogle County, had in his possession a large amount of money that he had recently received from the State of New York. This information was communicated to the gang by their friends at Washington Grove, in Ogle County, and immediate preparations were made by them to secure this prize, the amount of which was said to be about fourteen thousand dollars.

To accomplish this it was decided to be most advisable to commit the robbery under the cover of night. Minute information being necessary, one of the gang under the assumed name of Harris, visited the house for the avowed purpose of obtaining employment. Mr. Mulford wished to hire for six months, but Harris declined to engage for a longer term than three months, and there was some difference in opinion between them about wages. Harris, after some further conversation during which he carefully looked around, left with a promise to call again in a few days. How well he kept that promise the sequel will show!

A few nights after this three men entered the house of Mr. Mulford, disguised and fully armed with pistols and knives. Immediately on their entrance one seized a loaded rifle belonging to Mulford, that was standing in one corner of the room, and aiming it at his head, threatened him with instant death if he attempted to move or speak, and at the same time demanded his money. His wife also, who was by his side, was threatened in case she attempted to give any alarm or raise from her pillow.

Mr. Mulford told the robbers that he had but little money and where it was concealed. This, amounting to about four hundred dollars, they eagerly seized, and then by threats of instant death, attempted to make him give them the large sum they thought in his possession. Again and again he assured them that he had given them all he had, but thinking that he was deceiving them they began to search the house. The one who had the rifle remained at the bedside of Mr. and Mrs. Mulford as a guard, another stationed himself at the door, while the third whom Mrs. Mulford recognized as Harris, searched every part of the house.

Like an old and experienced hand in such matters, Harris allowed nothing to escape him, and even went so far as to bring several large cakes of tallow from the cellar and cut each completely apart, with a stroke of his large bowie knife, in order to satisfy himself that they did not contain money. A bureau in the room of Mrs. Mulford contained a large quantity of linen neatly folded and arranged, and this also was carefully searched by Harris, who shook each piece out to see that no money was secreted in it, and then threw it carelessly upon the floor.

Notwithstanding the perilous situation in which she was placed, and with death surrounding her on every side, Mrs. Mulford could not quietly see her linen, after the trouble it had cost her to arrange it, thrown into such disorder, and careless of the result, addressed the robber :

" Mr. Harris," said she, " you conduct yourself very differently from what you did the other day when you wished to obtain employment."

The unveiled robber sprang to his feet with a loud oath surprised at the daring of the defenceless and heroic woman. With eyes flashing with rage he sprang to the bedside and drawing his bowie knife waived it above her head.

" Lay down and cover up your head ! If you utter another word while we are in the house, I will make a stain on the floor that will last long after you are gone !"

Then t rning to his comrades, he continued in an under tone, and one in which fear was plainly distinguished.

"Boys, I must be missing. I'm known, and this is no place for me. A minute more, and I'm off."

The search was hastily finished, and the robbers left the house with the exception of Harris, who remained for a moment behind and addressed Mr. Mulford.

"Old man, do you intend to follow us?"

"I don't know," was the reply.

"Do you intend to follow us, I say?"

"I can't tell. I have not thought about it."

"You must tell. What do you say, old man?"

"I don't know that it will do any good."

"You had better not! Take my advice and keep still. There are a good many of us, and you could not catch us if you were to try. We shall leave a man with a loaded rifle to guard your door, and if any one ventures out before sunrise a bullet will end their prying. Good bye, old man, we are off, and you follow if you dare!"

With this parting salutation the robbers left, and Mr. Mulford after remaining perfectly quiet for a short time ventured out doors, but could see nothing of his late and unwelcome visitors. In the morning he gave the alarm, and a minute search was made, but without avail. Nothing could be learned in regard to them, and after a short time the matter was almost forgotten in the series of depredations that followed.

In the spring of 1844, a man in disguise entered the store of Mr. McKinney at Rockford, Illinois, during the night, and took from behind the counter a trunk containing about seven hundred dollars, with which he was about leaving, when the clerk, a brother of Mr. McKinney, who was sleeping on the counter, awoke, and demanded:

"Who is there?"

" Your brother wants the trunk," was the reply.

" But who are you?"

" Your brother wants the trunk."

" But stop! the trunk can't go. Who sent you for it?"

" Look here," replied the robber, taking the clerk by the hand, and drawing the keen edge of a bowie knife lightly across his fingers: " Do you feel that? it is very sharp, and I do not fear to use it! Keep still and you shan't be hurt, but *the trunk must go!*"

The clerk, finding that he was completely in the power of the ruffian, and that resistance would be vain, suffered the robber to depart with his prize, without molestation. Immediately, however, he alarmed the neighborhood and search was made, but neither the robber nor trunk could be found. The following day, the trunk was found a short distance from the store broken open and rifled of its contents, but no trace of the robber could be discovered—another daring and unatoned-for crime, to be charged to the desperate Banditti of the Prairies.

In the fall of 1844, a pedlar by the name of Miller was robbed of a large amount of goods at Troy Grove, but as usual the robbers remained undetected. A short time after, an attempt was made to rob a man near Inlet Grove, by two men who entered the house at night disguised and armed. One of the robbers feigned lameness, and perfectly imitated one Bliss at Inlet Grove, and the other was recognized as Dewey of the same place. Both were arrested, tried and convicted at the Spring term of the Lee County Circuit Court, and furnished with lodgings and employment at the expense of the State for the term of three years.

Soon after the conviction, a train of suspicious circumstances led to the arrest of a man named West, at Inlet

Grove, for the robbery of the pedlar at Troy Grove. Search was made, and wonderful as it may appear, a portion of the goods were found in his house.

West was committed to await his trial at the next term of the Court, but after remaining in prison a short time he offered to turn State's evidence and disclose all he knew concerning the gang. This proposition was accepted, and he made what he called a full confession and disclosure, impli cating a large number of men who were suspected, as well as many who had been heretofore watched. Upon these disclosures, several arrests were made, and some property that had been before stolen, recovered. Part of the goods that had been taken from the pedlar at Troy Grove were in the house of one Sawyer at Inlet, who was arrested, tried, convicted and sentenced to the Penitentiary for two years.

West accused one Fox, alias Sutton, and John Baker of having committed the robbery at Troy Grove, and said that most of the goods had been secreted at Inlet Grove, and subsequently taken to Iowa. He also avowed that Fox and Birch, alias Blecker, alias Harris, committed the robbery for which Bliss and Dewey were sent to prison, and that the former was totally innocent, while the latter was accessory, having " got up the sight." He further stated, that Fox had robbed one Mr. Hascal, a merchant at Inlet, by entering the house during a very severe thunder storm, and crawling upon the floor till he reached the trunk wherein was deposited the money, and having secured it, left without being heard, although Mr. and Mrs. Hascal were lying in the bed *awake*, at the time. To prove this, Fox subsequently stated the conversation that had passed between them while he was in the act of rifling the trunk!

These disclosures of West led to the arrest of Bridge and Oliver, who were convicted as accessory to the robbery of Mulford, and sentenced to the Penitentiary, one for seven and the other for eight years. He also revealed many particulars relative to the robbery of the stage of Messrs. Frink, Walker & Co., and the plot in regard to the Dixon Land Office, and after attending several terms of Court as a witness, and being instrumental in some convictions, left the country of his disgrace and villainy, it is thought, forever.

In the fall of 1844, two men traveling as Mormon preachers, stopped with a man of the Mormon faith near Pekin, on the Illinois River, stayed several days and preached in the neighborhood. One of them exchanged a hundred dollar bill with the old man, telling him that Brigham Young wanted the gold to purchase materials for the temple at Nauvoo, that could not be obtained for any other kind of money. By this exchange they ascertained where the old man kept his money, which amounted to nearly two thousand dollars, mostly in gold, and marked it for their prey. After remaining a few days longer, another of their comrades joined them and the three left their pious friend with many thanks for his hospitality, and good wishes for the cause of Mormonism. Little time, however, had escaped ere one of them returned, and entering the old man's house in the night, took every cent of money he possessed, including the hundred dollar bill he had kindly exchanged for them, and made his escape undiscovered.

Early in the spring of 1845, three men carefully disguised, entered the dwelling of a Norwegian family in Lee County, Iowa, during the dark hours of night, fully armed and prepared for robbery and bloodshed. With fearful oaths and imprecations, they demanded money. The terrified family gave the robbers all they possessed, but which, however, amounted to but a few dollars.   Disbelieving the word of the terrified ones, they proceeded to search the house, but without success, and having found a quantity of provisions ready cooked, they supped with much composure, and then, taking a quantity of clothing, left the house.

Soon after this, a Mr. Smith was robbed in a similar manner, in the same county, and apparently (from their operations) by the same band, and yet no clue could be obtained as to who they were, although Mr. Smith and his family were confident that they could recognize the robbers if they could see them.

Briefly have we sketched a few of the most daring robberies that were successfully carried through in the surrounding country, and that but to relate the *facts*, without embellishment, and now turn to what is of deeper interest, praying patience for the uninteresting style of our narrative.

CHAPTER II.

NAUVOO, the head-quarters of the Mormon chief and his satellites, had already increased to a population of sixteen or eighteen thousand. The great temple, which by the way, was built for the purpose of a fort or stronghold, was in process of erection, and rapidly being pushed on towards completion. Like the old established system of England, each member was required, aye, even compelled to give one-tenth of all he possessed, and annually thereafter give one-tenth of their income to the leaders of the church. The male members were also required to labor one-tenth of the time upon the temple or pay an equivalent therefor, in case of failure in money, to the amount of such labor to the temple committee. A rod of iron—a scepter of might was held constantly over their heads to enforce these things, and woe betide the man who dare disobey the arbitrary mandates of that church militant.

While the Mormons were rapidly increasing in numbers, and daily increasing their power and wealth, the country around was suffering severely from a succession of robberies almost without a parallel in the annals of crime. Stock of every description and goods of all kinds were constantly taken, and all in the vicinity trembled lest they like their neighbors, might be stripped of their all without a hope of restoration or revenge.

The offenders were frequently tracked in the direction of Nauvoo, and sometimes, though rarely, the property was recovered, but in no case could the perpetrators of the crime be arrested and brought to justice. In case of an arrest at Nauvoo the accused were immediately released by the city authorities, and the cry of "*Persecution against the Saints*" raised, effectually drowning the pleas for justice, of the injured, and the officer forced to return and tell the tale of defeat. This done, the fugitive found a safe shelter under the wide-spread wings of the Mormon leaders and laughed at pursuit.

Repeated threats were made by the robbed and injured, and as often answered by the cry of " Persecution against the Saints!" This cry was responded to from abroad by those who knew nothing of the real cause of complaint, with sympathy for the " poor, persecuted Mormons," and bitter denunciations against their persecutors who were the *real* sufferers and *most* deserving of sympathy. Thus affairs stood while still worse grew the troubles, and the bud of revenge was bursting into blossom. Even among themselves, the seeds of discord were planted, and bitter words were telling that even " Saints" were not perfection, whatever they might claim for themselves, or whoever were their leaders.

In the spring of 1844, Wm. Law, a leading Mormon, openly charged the Prophet (Joseph Smith) with an attempt to seduce his wife. (This soon after became the spiritual wife doctrine, and was believed, and even preached to some extent by the leaders of the Mormon Church.) This charge was promptly denied bv the Prophet, and Law was denounced in the most bitter terms for an alleged attempt to slander the Prophet—the holy head of the Church, and as a persecutor of the Saints. Summoned by the high tribunal of the Church, Law appeared, refused to retract what he had said, and again avowed its truth, for which he was immediately cut off from the Church. Being a man of considerable influence, Law drew with him a few of the disaffected members of the Church, who were already tired of bowing in humble submission, and paying tribute to the Prophet Joseph, and being held the ready subjects of his will and pleasure.

Among these deserters were Wilso, Law, Frank, Higby, Foster, and others, who determined to put the world in possession of their grievances, by publishing a long train of corruption and crimes, countenanced and practiced by the Prophets and heads of the Church, in which they had long been accomplices or accessory. In order more effectually to accomplish their designs and bring themselves into notice, they at once set about establishing a principal office at Nauvoo, in direct opposition to the will and special edict of the Prophet.

In the month of May, A. D. 1844, the new press was put in operation, and the prospectus and first number of a newspaper published under the title of the " Nauvoo Expositor." It contained a series of charges against Joseph Smith, and the leading men in the church, including bigamy, adultery, larceny, counterfeiting, &c. In reply to this, the " Nauvoo Neighbor," a newspaper printed under the direction and control of the Prophet, charged the dissenters from the Mormon faith with the same crimes, and sustained many of the charges by the publication of numerous affidavits, made, without doubt, by the Prophet's *standing witnesses.* Each

appeared determined to out-do the other in the promul-
gation of slander and abuse, with which, according to their
own stories, each had long possessed a knowledge of. If
either were guilty of half they were accused of, the gallows
had long been defrauded of its just dues, and earth was
teeming with the base, the vile, and the blood-stained.

But while the surrounding country was suffering by and
remonstrating against the prepetration of these crimes, and
charging them justly upon the Mormons, they with one
united voice echoed the cry of " Persecution for Righteous-
ness' sake." Then was it that the old adage was freely
proved, that when "rogues fall out honest men get their
dues."

Upon the issue of the first number of the " Expositor,"
the Prophet and his adherents determined to at once silence
them by the destruction of the press, and the total annihila-
tion of the office. The subject was brought before the City
Council, and many inflammatory speeches were made, in most
of which the members of the said Council participated. Smith,
the Prophet, told them " that the time had come to strike the
blow! That God no longer required them to submit to the
oppression of their enemies, and that he should vote for the
destruction of the press; that it was a nuisance, and he
should order it destroyed as such!"

Hiram Smith spoke in substance the same as his brother,
and also denounced in unmeasured terms, Sharp, the editor
of the Warsaw Signal. He said " he would give any man
five hundred dollars who would go into the Signal office
with a sledge and demolish the press. That it should be
done at all hazards, even if it took his farm to pay for it!"

Upon calling for the vote, eleven voted for, and one
against, declaring the Expositor a nuisance, and immediate

measures were taken for carrying the ordinance of its destruction into effect. This dissenting vote was a Mr. Warring, and the only anti-Mormon in the Council, and little was he regarded by the hot-headed ones who were bent on destruction.

The City Marshal, acting under the orders of the Council, raised a force of several hundred men, headed by Gen. Dunham of the Nauvoo Legion, armed with clubs, &c., and proceeded to the printing office. Meeting with no resistance, they entered the office, took the blank paper and other materials and burned them in the street, pied the type, and taking the press into the street, broke it into pieces with hammers.

This done, they repaired to the house of the Prophet, who addressed them in terms of praise, applauding them for their services, and telling them that they had but done their duty and upheld the law. In return he was loudly cheered by the mob, after which they quietly and immediately dispersed. Some of the leaders, however, remained and congratulated each other upon their success, and the downfall of the power of their enemies. Foremost among them was the Marshall, who thus addressed the Prophet:

" General, this is the happiest hour of my life!"

" Thank you, my good fellow," was the reply, " you have done well, done your *duty*, and shall be rewarded for it."

This outrage upon the public press helped to fan the flame already kindled against the Mormon outlaws, by their repeated depredations upon the citizens of the surrounding country, and plainly foreshadowed the storm that was to burst with startling fury.

The dissenting Mormons at once united with those opposed to that sect, and various meetings were called, and all

2

parties urged to arm and prepare themselves to resist any
further aggression: to be ready at all hazards to protect
themselves and meet the worst. Warrants were issued
against the Smiths, and other leaders, in the destruction of
the printing office of the Expositor, and though served by
the proper officers, they refused to obey the mandates of the
law, and laughed at its power!

As in all former cases, the writ of habeas corpus was
resorted to, and all the arrested at once set at liberty and
discharged from arrest; the same persons that were arrested
acting as officers of the Courts that discharged them! Thus
effectually defeating the ends of justice, and compelling the
officer to return to Carthage without a single prisoner!

This mock administration of law, added new fuel to the
flame. The public being convinced that Nauvoo was the
headquarters of nearly all the marauders who were preying
upon the surrounding community, together with the full belief that the Mormon leaders were privy to their depredations, and the resistance and defeat of justice, now became
enraged, and determined to rise in their might and enforce
the law, even though it should be at the point of the bayonet or sabre. Determined to rid themselves of the harpies
that were gnawing at their very vitals, and if need be, rid
themselves of the whole Mormon population. Thoroughly
aroused, and conscious not only of their power but also the
justice of their cause, they fearlessly avowed their purposes,
and though still defying, the most secret recesses of Mor-
mondom trembled in view of the bursting of the tempest
they had raised, but could not avert.

The officer, from whose custody the Smiths and others
were discharged, proceeded to summon a posse and renew
the arrest from the adjacent counties, rallied under the ban-

ner of law and justice. The Mormon leaders learning this
fact, gathered also their forces. The Nauvoo Legion, organized at the call of the Prophet, fully armed and equipped
and numbering nearly four thousand, with their pieces of
artillery, prepared for a desperate resistance.

The City of Nauvoo was declared under martial law, and
all necessary preparations were made to sustain the edicts of
the Prophet and the freedom of the crime-stained ones, or
die in the attempt.

The officer, finding his force, or posse, far inferior to that
of the Mormons, called upon the Governor of the State for
aid to enforce the law and allow right, for a time, to triumph
over might. Governor Ford, learning the true state of affairs in Hancock County, immediately ordered out several
companies of State troops, and repaired with them, in person, to suppress the disturbances, and enforce the law. On
his arrival, he proceeded to examine into the causes of the
difficulty, and despatched a messenger to Nauvoo, requiring
the Prophet, Smith, to send a deputation to meet him at
Carthage, and explain the conduct of the Mormons. Smith
appointed John Taylor, one of the twelve apostles of the
Church, and Dr. Burnhisle, a leading Mormon, to wait on
the Governor.

A full investigation was entered into, and Gov. Ford, in-
structing the officer having the writs from which the Mormons had discharged themselves, to proceed to Nauvoo and
demand the surrender of the Smiths and others upon whom
the writs had already been served, and in case of a refusal
to obey the law, to enforce it at the point of the bayonet.
At the same time pledging himself, as the Chief Executive
of the State, to protect them from personal violence, and

the troops under his command pledged themselves to sustain him.

The officer with a sufficient guard set off for Nauvoo,
having also an order to disband the Nauvoo Legion, which
on his arrival was disbanded. The several persons named
in the writs, also agreed to accompany him on the following
morning without trouble : and how well it would have
been, had their promise been faithfully kept.

Morning came, and the hour of their departure arrived,
but the Prophet could not be found, having crossed the
Mississippi river during the night with his brother Hiram,
and secreted themselves in Iowa, and the officer was again
forced to return to Carthage without the prisoners.

Nauvoo was again a scene of confusion, all the inhabitants taking part in the trouble. Some rejoicing at the
escape of the Prophet, while others were loud in their
curses, avowing that he had deserted them, in the hour of
danger left them to the mercy of their enemies, and was the
cause of all their difficulty.

Smith before leaving had instructed his wife to take her
children, with the family of his brother Hiram, on board
the steamer " Maid of Iowa," then lying at the foot of Main
street ready for departure, and leave the city. With these
instructions, however, she refused to comply, and remained
at home.

During the day, several despatches crossed the river to
and from the Prophet; some advising him to seek safety in
flight, and others urging him to return and save the city.
Thus urged, the Prophet and his companion in flight,
re-crossed the river about sunset, and on the following
morning started for Carthage, and Nauvoo was again quiet.
When within a few miles of Carthage, they were met by a

detachment of State troops on their way to Nauvoo to demand the State arms there in possession of the Nauvoo Legion. The Smiths immediately retraced their steps, delivered up the arms on the order of the Governor, and again left for Carthage on the morning of the 26th of June.

On arriving there, the prisoners were examined on the charge of riot in destroying the printing press, and held to bail for their appearance at the next term of the Hancock Circuit Court. Joseph and Hiram Smith were arrested on charge of treason, and committed to await their examination.

All being tranquil, and Governor Ford thinking an armed force no longer necessary disbanded his troops on the morning of the 27th, leaving but a small force to guard the jail, and proceeded with his suite to Nauvoo. Here he addressed the Mormons, urging upon them the necessity of observing and upholding the laws; preserving order, and respecting the rights of their fellow citizens, and telling them the inevitable result of a continuance of their former course of conduct.

After the troops were disbanded, the most hostile of them, believing the Smiths eventually would be acquitted on the charge of treason, and the Mormons, still continued their depredations, and deeming that the only way to secure safety was by ridding them of their leaders, they still continued to fan the flame of revenge that had heretofore been burning but too brightly. Urged on by the Mormon dissenters, who were thirsting for blood, they collected, to the number of about one hundred and forty, armed and disguised, and proceeded to the jail about five o'clock in the afternoon of the 27th. Having dispersed the guard, they attacked the jail, and Joseph and Hiram Smith in an effort to escape were both shot dead. Four balls pierced each of them, and any one of the wounds would have proved fatal. Having accomplished this cold-blooded murder, (for surely no other name will apply to it,) and glutted their appetite for blood, the mob instantly dispersed.

Great indeed has been the provocation, and revenge had been nursed and fostered by a long series of injuries, and yet they can, as we look calmly at the past, but little atone for the blood shed on that night, the breaking of the law and the wanton sacrifice of human life on the fearful altar of the human passions.

Post haste from Carthage, whose streets were now stained with blood, a messenger was despatched to Nauvoo, with the news of this double murder, who met Gov. Ford and suite on his return from Nauvoo, and a few miles from that city.

The Governor hastened to Carthage, and fearing that the Mormons would rise in force, massacre the citizens and burn the city, advised the immediate evacuation of the town. Most of the inhabitants fled in disorder, fearful that to avenge the death of their leaders, the Mormons would spare none. Gov. Ford, having placed General Demming in command of a small body of troops, with instructions to guard the town, and watch the movements of the Mormons, proceeded at once to Quincy, a distance of about fifty miles.

The effect upon the Mormons was far different from what had been anticipated, for, apparently disheartened by the loss of their leaders, no effort at revenge was made. Sad, silent and gloomy, they seemed to brood over the past, rather than to think of violence, and all remained quiet.

The bodies of the deceased were conveyed to Nauvoo on the 28th, and met at the entrance of the city by a large concourse of people of both sexes and all ages, who followed them to the late residence of the Prophet. Here they were addressed by several prominent men of their Church, and exhorted to keep from all violence, and quietly submit to the persecution of their enemies.

All remained quiet for a few weeks, during which time the Mormons re-organized, acknowledging the twelve apostles to be at the head of the Church. The building of the temple and other public works were resumed, and again security and peace were felt by all.

Soon, however, complaints from the surrounding country told that the ruffians were again at work, and as heretofore, all attempts to bring the offenders to justice proved abortive. If arrested, witnesses were always ready to swear them clear, and all again was in a state of disorder and fear. The smouldering fires were again ready to burst forth, and riot and bloodshed take the place of law and order. Another tragedy was to be enacted, fearful and bloody, and another victim sent unprepared into the presence of his Maker.

CHAPTER III.

THE MURDER OF MILLER AND LIECY.

ON the night of the 10th of May, 1845, a most barbarous and bloody murder was committed in Lee County, Iowa, about twelve miles from Nauvoo, and three and one half from West Point, the county seat of Lee County, startling and affrighting all.

To properly understand the sequel, it will be necessary for us briefly to explain the circumstances prior to the deed of blood.

About the 25th of the previous April, Mr. John Miller with his son-in-law emigrated from the State of Ohio, located himself in Lee County, and offered to pay cash for a good farm. It was reported that he was possessed of a large sum of money, and at once he was marked as a prey by the lawless and blood-stained ones.

A few days after this, two strangers appeared in the neighborhood, who said they had just moved into that part of the country and were searching for an ox they had lost. They described him fully, and made particular inquiries as well as indirect ones about the settlers in the vicinity. They staid at a house about one-fourth of a mile from Miller's one night, and the next morning went to Miller's and endeavored to get a bank note changed, alleging that they wanted the change to pay for their lodging.

About twelve or one o'clock on the night of the 10th of May, three men entered the house of Miller, armed with pistols, bowie-knives and clubs. In the room there were three beds spread upon the floor.

The one in the northeast corner was occupied by Mr. and Mrs. Liecy, the one in the northwest corner by Mr. and Mrs. Miller, and the third, at the north side of the room, by a man and his wife, whose name is not recollected. Upon entering the room, one of the ruffians opened a dark lantern, the light from which reflected upon the two beds occupied by Miller and Liecy, and immediately jumped upon the table, while the other two advanced to their bedsides. Each with a heavy club aimed a deadly blow at his victim, injuring them severely, but not so as to keep them from springing to their feet before receiving a second. Grasping those who were intent on taking their lives, a desperate struggle ensued. Immediately the lantern was closed, and its holder sprang to the assistance of his companions in crime.

For several minutes the struggle continued amid the cries and shrieks of the terrified women, and the groans of their husbands as they were stabbed and cut by the deadly bowie knives of their assassins, while they, unarmed, sought to repel them, and struggled almost hopelessly for life.

It was a fearful struggle, against fearful odds, but bravely and well were the murderers met. At length Mr. Miller, by a desperate effort, succeeded in pushing his antagonist from the house, and hope sprang up in his breast. Vain, however, was its cherishing power, for as he passed the door the knife of the remorseless robber pierced his side, and entered his heart! With a single groan he reeled, stag-

gered, and fell to the ground never to rise again: another
victim to the Banditti of the Prairies.

Liecy succeeded in throwing over one of the ruffians upon
the floor, and while in the act of choking him the knife of
the other was inflicting deep gashes upon his head, and
piercing frightfully his back. Desperately he battled, but
maddened by pain and becoming very weak from the loss
of blood, he with one effort freed himself from their hold
and gained his feet. One effort more and he forced them
through the open door, and strove to close it. Already it
was closing and in another moment he would be safe! Oh!
the happiness of that thought! But see, a flash glances on
the air of midnight, the whizzing of a bullet is heard, and
pierced by a ball, when on the very verge of safety, he sinks
helpless upon the floor.

The third man, during that soul-affrightening struggle,
remained quietly in his bed, secreting himself under the
cover, and allowed his friends to be cruelly murdered without a single effort to save them! Uninjured, except from
fright: he was a very coward and a craven!

The assassins, becoming alarmed at the manner in which
they had been met, and fearing that the shrieks of the
women and the report of the pistols might alarm the neighborhood, left without securing their booty. Blood-stained,
and branded like Cain, were they, and fled under the cover
of night to find safety from all but the terrors of a goading
conscience.

As soon as the family had recovered sufficiently from
fright to allow reason to again occupy her usurped domin-
ion, they despatched a messenger to West Point, where the
district court was in session. The news created great
excitement, and a large number of citizens together with

the Sheriff repaired at once to the scene of the murder, when a horrid spectacle was presented to their shuddering vision.

In the front yard and within a few feet of the door, lay Mr. Miller, cold and lifeless, his head, inclining to the right, upon descending ground, which was stained for a considerable distance with blood. A ghastly stream, now chilled and waveless! Entering the house, they found Mr. Liecy lying upon the floor weltering in blood, and apparently in the agonies of death. Everything presented, at a single glance, a perfect scene of carnage. The floor was stained and spotted with the ruddy stream of life, horrid for the eye to rest upon, affrighting the very soul, bidding the pulse stand still and the heart forget its office. The groans and cries of the afflicted family, as they burst from trembling and pallid lips, helped to complete the fearful tragedy and appal the beholders, telling how fearfully the fiends had completed their mission of death.

Surgical aid was immediately procured, but uselessly, for upon examination the wounds that the survivor had received were pronounced fatal. The skull was pierced and broken by the strokes of the heavy bowie knife, and it had deeply buried itself in his back. The ball received upon the doorstep was extracted, after having passed quite through his body, and became flattened against the bones. Though Mr. Liecy's decease was hourly expected, yet he survived long enough to see in irons and identify the perpetrators of the dark and hellish deed.

Every effort was made by James L. Estes, sheriff of Lee County, and others, to arrest the murderers, and bring them to justice. The news spread with lightning-like rapidity, and the particulars were soon in every mouth. The citi-

zens of the surrounding country turned out " en masse,"
organized themselves into companies, and scoured the
country in hopes of obtaining some clue to the perpetrators
of the fiendish outrage against both the laws of God and
man.

In searching the premises a cloth cap was found, trimmed
with fur, and without a front-piece, being the only clue
that might lead to the identity of the villains. This was
carefully preserved as a silent witness in case of need.
Tracks were found leading from the house across a ploughed
field into a road, in the direction of Nauvoo. These were
followed by Sheriff Estes to within a few miles of the said
city, when all traces were lost.

The news of this murder reached Montrose, where I
resided, on the morning of the murder, at about ten o'clock.
The citizens turned out, and the search became general.
Every ravine, thicket and bluff was searched, but without
success, for a day or two, when the citizens returned discouraged to their homes, believing that the perpetrators of this
crime would, like all others, escape justice.

Having heard of the cap that had been found at the house,
with a full description of it, I at once recollected having
seen a young man in Nauvoo some three weeks previous by
the name of Hodges, with a cap of the same description. I
communicated this information immediately to Sheriff Estes,
and learned from him that the Hodges were known as men
of suspicious characters. In the meantime, I discovered
several persons standing about the streets of Montrose
eagerly listening to all the plans and movements against the
murderers, and anxious to learn who, if any, were suspected.
The excitement having passed away, and the sheriff's posse
dispersed, and all again had become quiet, I determined to
track up, as the first step towards an arrest, the *fatal cap*

I immediately left for Nauvoo on the afternoon of the 12th, and commenced such inquiries as would tend to remove or confirm the suspicions against the Hodges, and found that three of the Hodges, Amos, William and Stephen, were living together in a retired part of the city. Amos being married, the others were boarding with him, and all were without any visible means of subsistence. That on the afternoon of the 10th, William and Stephen Hodges and Thomas Brown were seen passing up in a skiff towards the mouth of Devil Creek, in the direction the murder was committed. Early in the morning of the 11th, one of the Hodges was seen going from the river towards his home *bare-headed*, and since that time had worn a hat, although he had previously worn a *cap*. On the 11th, Stephen Hodges was seen in a grocery in Nauvoo with a drop of blood on the bosom of his shirt, and being questioned in regard to it made no reply, but went immediately home and returned with a clean one.

These circumstances more than confirmed the suspicions already excited by the description of the cap, and I determined, if possible, to arrest them and investigate the subject. Acting upon this determination, I called upon S. Markham, Captain of the City Watch, and made known to him my business and asked his assistance. He cheerfully consented to aid me, said he had men who would do anything he told them, and that he would follow my direction in making the arrest.

He immediately called to his assistance eighteen or twenty men, armed for the purpose, and at two o'clock in the morning of the 13th, we proceeded to the residence of Hodges and surrounded the house. Markham rapped at the door, but no attention was paid to it. A slight noise was heard in the house, and a light appeared through the windows, and I saw three men in the house, each armed with a gun, and one of them put a bowie knife into his breast, and stepped to the door and demanded:

" Who is there?"

" I am," replied Markham

" You are Mr. Markham?"

" Yes."

" What do you want?"

" I want to come in."

" You cannot enter."

" I wish to see you."

" The first one that attempts to enter is a dead man."

" I wish to speak to you."

" What business have you here at this time of night."

" The citizens of Iowa have come over to arrest you, and I determined to get the start of them. You shall have a fair trial in the city, if you will surrender. Will you do so?"

" If you will wait till morning we will surrender."

After a few minutes of consultation we concluded to accept their proposition and guard the house until daylight and thus prevent all escape. We informed them of our determination and all remained quiet.

Daylight came, and Markham rapped at the door, when Amos opened it, and the three brothers surrendered without further resistance. They were taken before one Johnson, a Mormon Justice of the Peace, who agreed to hold them in custody until I could go to West Point and notify Sheriff Estes and return again. The Hodges manifested very little uneasiness and made no objection to the detention.

I left Nauvoo at 7 o'clock on the morning of the 13th, crossed the river to Montrose, proceeded to West Point, and

notified the sheriff of the arrest, who with several citizens
returned with me to Nauvoo, where we arrived on the evening of the same day and found the Hodges safe in custody.
Sheriff Estes made affidavit for a warrant, which being issued, they were legally arrested and remained for examination.   No evidence having been adduced against Amos
Hodges he was discharged.   Brown, who was also strongly
suspected, fled before sufficient evidence could be found
against him to justify his arrest.

CHAPTER IV.

THE TRIAL.

THE arrest of the Hodges had become public, and much excitement prevailed in the surrounding country, as well as in Nauvoo. Being Mormons, but little hopes were entertained by the community at large of detaining them in custody sufficient time to collect testimony and put them upon trial. Strong efforts were being constantly made in Nauvoo to ensure their acquittal on the examination, or effect their escape, and a large number of witnesses were collected for this purpose, ready to swear that they were in Nauvoo at the time the murder was committed.

With this strong array of testimony in their favor, and the Mormon influence before a Mormon magistrate, against the circumstantial evidence in our possession, there was little hope of our success. Indeed, all looked forward to an acquittal, although every circumstance tended strongly to confirm their guilt. Under this state of affairs, the matter was abandoned entirely to my arrangement.

" Bonney," said he, " you have made the arrest, and must conduct the examination. With this strong array of witnesses I fear they will get clear, although I have no doubt of their guilt. I can do nothing with these Mormons, and shall leave the affair to your skill and judgment, assisting you as much as I can."

Reluctantly I consented, and determined to make the best of a bad case, and, if possible, thwart their plans, set at defiance their army of " standing witnesses," and hold the Hodges to answer before a legal tribunal. I resorted to the following expedient.

On the following morning, at the hour set for the trial, the court-room was filled with witnesses for the prisoners, and dark indeed was the prospect of their being committed. Under pretence of procuring more testimony from Iowa, I applied for a continuance until the following day, which, after considerable opposition, was granted, and the time fixed at 10 o'clock, A. M.

I immediately determined to take all our witnesses that were in attendance and proceed to West Point, where the Lee County Grand Jury were in session, and procure a bill of indictment. This having been accomplished, my purpose was to return to Nauvoo with a certified copy, which would hold the prisoners, and await the requisition of the Governor, in despite the testimony of their friends.

While Sheriff Estes and myself were preparing to set out on this mission, the steamboat New Purchase arrived from Fort Madison loaded with passengers, amongst whom were several witnesses against the Hodges. Some of them recognized S. Hodges as one of the Ox hunters before spoken of, which, with other facts, were thought by the " knowing ones " to be sufficient to hold the Hodges, and all were eager for an immediate examination. I objected, but without assigning my reason, well believing that if my intentions were known by the Mormons, the escape of the prisoners would be certain, whilst their friends now doubted not that they would be sworn clear by their confederates.

3'

This being the case, we left at once for West Point, in direct opposition to the solicitation of our friends, where we arrived the same evening, and found the Grand Jury in session waiting our arrival, in compliance with the request of a messenger who had been previously despatched.

The witnesses were at once examined, and a bill of indictment found against Stephen and William Hodges, and Thomas Brown, for the murder of Miller, (Liecy being yet alive). A certified copy having been procured, we set out on our return, and arrived in Nauvoo in time to meet the Court of Examination at the appointed hour.

So great was the excitement that hundreds collected, both from Illinois and Iowa, and the streets were densely crowded. General Demming, the then Sheriff of Hancock County, was in attendance, and a steamer from Fort Madison brought a crowd of persons anxious to be present at the examination. Friends and foes alike were there, and on every face was depicted anxiety, fear, or hope.

The Court at last convened, and the prisoners arraigned for examination, with an array of witnesses, and defended by Almond Babit, Esq. After several attempts to still the dense crowd into silence, it was at length accomplished, and the examination began. Then the copy of the indictment was produced, effectually placing them beyond the reach of false witnesses bribed for the purpose. The court-room was at once a scene of confusion, such as the eye but seldom rests upon. The cheers of the friends of justice, and the loud curses of the others, commingled in one overwhelming din, and riot and bloodshed seemed the inevitable consequence. Wild indeed was the storm, and who could say whether it would subside or burst in fury? Completely disheartened, however, by this unlookedfor proceeding, baffled and outwitted, the friends of the Hodges quietly submitted, and the prisoners were held to await a requisition from Iowa.

All now seemed quiet, and yet the slightest cause would have resulted in the complete destruction of Nauvoo, and the expulsion of the Mormons, and great fears were entertained; the excited populace could not be restrained from acts of violence. The danger of their escape by the breaking of the jail, or rescue by their friends, was also feared, and deep and fearful revenge was avowed in either case, which added to the excitement already verging towards its height.

To guard against all danger, and still if possible the tumult, I suggested to the counsel for the prisoners, that, notwithstanding they protested their innocence, yet they must answer to the laws of their country under the indictment. If innocent they would not fear the result, and that in order to place themselves in safety beyond all hazards, that they surrender to the authorities of Iowa, and avoid the necessity of procuring a requisition. Mr. Babit, their counsel, favored this suggestion, and urged the prisoners to comply with the proposition, to which, after some consideration, they consented. Safely lodged in prison at Fort Madison, beyond the hope of rescue, or escape, the minds of the people of the surrounding country again became calm, and business, that had for a time been neglected, was again resumed.

Facts having been elicited during the investigation with regard to the Hodges, that proved conclusively that Thomas Brown was the third of the infamous three, I was urged by many to pursue, and if possible arrest him. Being legally authorized to offer a reward of five hundred dollars for his

arrest and delivery into my custody, in any State or Territory in the United States, I left to accomplish if possible
this mission, on the morning of the 28th May. On reaching
Quincy, I introduced my business to Sheriff Pitman, who
was an officer of great merit, and a perfect gentleman; and
who, in his official character, was extensively known to the
gang, as well as acquainted with their proceedings, which
enabled him to give me much valuable information.

Sheriff Pitman was well acquainted with the general
character of Brown, and knew several of his confederates
in crime, who lived on the Mississippi bottoms, in the north
part of Adams county, eighteen miles north of Quincy.
Amongst these was a Mr. Bingham, a relative of Brown's,
and who had served out one term in the penitentiary for
larceny. After gathering from him all necessary information and directions, I determined to visit the gang in the
neighborhood of Bingham, and by stratagem learn whether
secreted in the vicinity, and whether any of them knew
anything with regard to him.

I at once set out, and after riding till within a few miles
of the house of Bingham, I met a man on horseback of
whom I inquired for a Mr. Agard, to whom I had been
directed by Sheriff Pitman, as a person in whom I could
confide, and who would give me any information in his
power. He immediately replied:

" My name is Agard."

" The Sheriff of your county directed me to call on you."

" Oh! I suppose I know your business. You are in pursuit of the murderers of *Jo Smith.* Well, well, I suppose
I must go with you."

" That is not my business. The Sher—

" Oh! well sir, what did you want? "

"I was directed to you to inquire for a Mr. Bingham. I wish to find some land in his neighborhood."

"Oh! is that all? I can tell you all about Mr. Bingham, and the land in his township; I have a map and can inform you who owns every tract."

"Would you be kind enough to give me such information?"

"Yes, yes, at any time."

"When can you do it?"

"Why, to-morrow, I'll meet you at Mr. ——'s grocery, one and a half miles east of here, and give you any information you desire."

"I shall be obliged to you, sir."

After a few more remarks we separated, and on the following morning according to appointment I called at Mr. ——'s grocery, but without finding him. I learned, however, that the Hancock Circuit Court was in session, and that several persons were under arrest charged with the murder of the brothers Smith. Also, Mr. Agard had called early in the morning on Dr. ——, and told him "there was something wrong in the wind—that he had seen a stranger yesterday inquiring for land, but that he believed it only was a ruse and should keep himself out of sight."

Disappointed, but not disheartened, I continued my search, though unavailing, throughout the day, and on the following morning called at the house of Mr. Bingham, to whom I introduced myself by the name of "Morris."

"Is your name Bingham?"

"Yes, that is my name."

"I have heard of you, and would like to have a little confident conversation with you."

"Certainly. Upon what subject?"
4

" I am just from the eastern part of the State, where I
' raised' a horse, which I left below for sale, and thought I
would come up and see what was going on in the way of
business."

" I am glad you called, though we are all idle here at
present.   The boys up north, however, seem to have their
hands full."

" What is doing here?"

" They have made several good 'raises,' though I learn
some of them have got into rather a serious scrape."

" Scrape!   Of what kind?"

" They attempted to rob an old German by the name of
Miller, and in order to escape were obliged to murder both
him and his son-in-law."

" Serious business, truly."

" Yes, but that is not the worst of it."

" Why, is there anything more?"

" Two of them have been arrested, and I understand they
are after the third."

" That is bad luck.   But can they not get clear?"

" I don't know.   It is somewhat doubtful."

" Are you acquainted up the river?"

" Not much."

" You know the Mormons?"

" Yes, I was amongst them, and a Mormon myself."

" Do you know which of the boys were arrested for the
murder you have spoken of?"

" Two of the Hodges."

" I suppose they are guilty."

" No doubt of it.   They are hard cases."

" It will probably go hard with them."

" Yes, but they won't catch the third."

" The third!"

" Yes, Tom Brown. He is one of the hardest I know of. He does nothing but follow the business. I have seen him go into a store in the day time, and steal a roll of cloth and put out with it, and he makes a practice of going to St. Louis on one side of the river and coming back the other, raking down both ways."

" He must be an old hand?"

" They won't catch him. He is too smart for that."

" Was he engaged in the murder with the Hodges?"

" I presume he was."

" I should like to get acquainted with him. I think I could get him into an operation that would suit him."

" Very likely, he is ready for anything."

" Does he come here often?"

" Not very. I don't think he would suit you though."

" Why not?"

" He is too reckless."

" I want two of the boys who are of the right stripe to go to Shawneetown with me."

" What is the speculation?"

" To relieve an old Dutchman of a chest of specie."

" That's the kind of speculation that would suit him. I can't do much here. I am suspected and have to keep very quiet."

" Two would be enough, and I think with you and Brown, we could do the thing up right."

" I don't know where Tom is, but there is a man living about two miles from here, who is a first rate hand in such business."

" But suppose he could not go?"

" Oh there is plenty in this County who would be glad of such a chance "

Being satisfied that he did not know the whereabouts of Brown, I told him I was obliged to go to Missouri before I made the strike at Shawneetown, but would call on him when I returned, and make some arrangement with him, when he continued the conversation.

" Are you acquainted in Missouri? "

" No, not much."

" I can give you the points there, if you want them."

" I do, it helps me greatly."

" I have a brother on the Missouri River who is right, and knows all the Boys. If you get there you are safe. Tell him *I* sent you and it will be all right."

" I shall not forget him."

" When you come this way come and see me. I can secrete you, and hide your horse so that the devil himself cannot find him.

" But if I should want to run? "

" I keep a boat to cross the Mississippi, and can ferry my friends across at night as well as in the day time, and tell them where they can stop and be secure."

After wishing me success, and giving me a list of names with whom to stop in Missouri, I left him and returned to Quincy on the evening of the 23rd, and gave Sheriff Pitman the particulars of my interview with Bingham. Leaving there I proceeded to St. Louis, where I got traces of Brown, and searched until the morning of the 27th without further success. After making such arrangements with the City Marshal as would secure the arrest of Brown if he should visit St. Louis, I departed for Memphis. Searching fully there, assisted by William D. Pilmore, a constable who had been kindly detailed for that duty by the Mayor, and becoming satisfied that Brown was not to be found, I again left for St. Louis.

Brown had visited St. Louis during my short absence, and an unsuccessful attempt had been made to arrest him. This, as he would now be on his guard, rendered the task I had undertaken still more arduous and doubtful, yet still I determined to pursue it to the end—to victory or to death. But being now completely at fault, I knew not which way to proceed, and while in this state of suspense I received a letter from Sheriff Estes which determined me to return and attend the trial of the Hodges. Perfecting my arrangements with the City Marshal, I immediately left and arrived at Montrose on the evening of the 5th of June.

Stephen and William Hodges were removed to West Point from Fort Madison on the 20th of May, and arraigned for trial, but a change of venue was taken to Des Moines County, where they were now to suffer the penalty of the law, or come forth cleared of the worst crime whose name stains the statute book.

Mr. Liecy, who was still alive, though rapidly sinking from the effects of his wounds, was confident that he could identify his murderers, if he was permitted to see them. In order to add his testimony to that of the others, Sheriff Estes selected persons who were strangers to Liecy, and who nearest resembled the Hodges, and took them to the residence of Liecy. They were seated in a circle in the room of the dying man, when, after a careful survey of their size, features, and general appearance, he singled out Stephen Hodges, saying:

" That is the man who stabbed me with the bowie knife."

" Another look round the circle and he pointed to William Hodges:

" That is the man who shot me ! "

Many questions were asked him in order to test the strength of his belief, but he wavered not for a single moment, or in the least controverted his assertions. Strong testimony this, falling as it did, from the lips of one who would soon pass through the gates of death, and it was fully confirmed by Mrs. Miller and Mrs. Liecy.

Other evidence also came to light by which the Hodges were tracked from Nauvoo to the scene of the daring murder, and back again to that city, and a pistol was found in their possession, the ball of which corresponded in size and weight with the one taken from the body of Liecy. How true it is, that murder may be tracked to the hand that did the deed, and is stained in blood, by the smallest and apparently most immaterial circumstances.

Monday, the 8th of June, was the day fixed for the trial, and the friends of the prisoners having become alarmed, made every effort in their power to secure their acquittal. Erwin Hodges, the brother, who was residing about thirty-one miles from Nauvoo, was the most active, took the lead in arranging their plan of defence, and swore bitter and deadly vengeance against all who took part in their arrest or prosecution. Being also a Mormon, he denounced the leaders of the Church for suffering his brothers to be taken out of Nauvoo, and said if they were hung it should cost the best blood in that city.

Messrs. Hall & Mills of Burlington, Iowa, were employed to defend them, and their fee of one thousand dollars secured to them. All that could be done to prevent a verdict of guilty, was carefully thought of and carried through, as a

primary step towards this end, and affidavit for a continu-
ance was filed, sworn to by the Hodges, to obtain the follow-
ing witnesses: John and Aaron Long, Judge Fox and
Henry Adams of St. Louis, and John W. Braffit, Henry
Moore, Samuel Smith, Lydia Hodges, John Bliss, Caroline
Moore, Samuel Walton, Sarah Ann Wood, Horace Braffit,
Mrs. Artemus Johnson, Thomas Morgan, (a son of the late
William Morgan of Batavia, N. Y., author of disclosures on
Masonry,) John Court, Mrs. Campbell, (sister of the
Hodges,) Harriet St. John, and a Miss Hawkins of Nauvoo;
witnesses not then present, who would swear that they
were in Nauvoo at the time of the murder, and other facts
that would establish their innocence beyond the power of
contradiction.

On this affidavit the case was continued until the 15th of
the same month, during which time I remained at Montrose, and occasionally visited Nauvoo, to watch the movements of those whose names were inserted in the said affidavit. Everything tended to confirm the former opinion of
both Sheriff Estes and myself that they were all connected
with the same gang, and intended to swear their comrades
out at all hazards. But suspicion was not testimony, and
nothing remained for us to do but to watch and bide our
time.

The anxiously looked-for day of trial came, and armed
with good counsel on either side, the trial began. By a
strong chain of circumstantial evidence, a clear case was
made out against the prisoners, backed by the testimony of
the wives of the murdered men, and the assertions of Liecy
as to their identity, which he reiterated in the last moments of
his life. A vigorous defence was made, but the witnesses
for the prisoners could not tell a consistent story, and fre-

quently gave the lie one to the other, though all agreed that they were in Nauvoo at the time the murder was committed. In this they had been well *trained*, but those who tutored them forgot to designate any particular point, and consequently, some swore to one point and others to another. This alone was sufficient to controvert their testimony in this particular, and show the object for which they were brought there.

Lydia Hodges, wife of Amos Hodges, who was in attendance as a witness, feigned sickness, and was absent from the court room and sent for one of the counsel for the prisoners. As he entered the room she burst into tears, and exclaimed:

" Must I go to court? "

" If you can swear the Boys were at home, on the night of the murder, your testimony will be very material and cannot be dispensed with.   Can you swear that? "

" They were out that night."

" Do you know where they were? "

" They left home in company with Tom Brown, and said they were going over to Iowa? "

" When did they return? "

" Early the next morning."

" What did they say? "

" That they had been unsuccessful."

" And nothing about the murder? "

" They said that they had a desperate fight, and were afraid that they had killed somebody."

" What is their business? "

" Robbery is the only one I know of."

" Who are engaged with them? "

" All their father's family, and leaders in the Mormon Church encourage them in it, and share the spoils."

"You know all this, or is it merely a rumor?"

"I know it, and am now brought here to swear them clear. They have always been kind to me, and yet I cannot swear my soul to eternal perdition, and destroy all my hopes of happiness both here and hereafter, to save them. Must I go to Court?"

"I don't know yet."

"I cannot, will not, do it! I cannot swear for them, and I will not swear against them."

Other conversation was had, and the lawyer returned again to Court, more than ever convinced of the hopelessness of his case, though he still struggled hard to the very end. It was vain, however, for after much time had been consumed in the trial, it was brought to a close by the fearful word that fell from the lips of the foreman of the jury—the end at once of their hopes, and the consummation of their fears, the knell of the tocsin of death—the dreadful word—GUILTY!

A horrid sound, is it not, to fall upon the ear of man? What phantoms rise at it—the rope, the gibbet, the coffin, the grave! Show me the eye that can look calmly upon them, and the heart that does not grow sick, and the form that does not tremble aspenlike at the bare mention of their horrors. How then must it be when they know that each day brings them nearer, and each turn of the hand upon the dial is hastening them to their certain doom? Awful! awful!! and yet "blood for blood" is the cry, and a waving sea of human hands surround the place of execution, unsatisfied and restless, till the last gasp attests the passage of the soul from earth.

Strong efforts were made by their brother, Erwin Hodges, to arouse the Mormons, and urge them to attempt

their rescue. Loudly he threatened and swore that if Brigham Young did not send men to break open the jail and
save them he would denounce them to the proper authorities, and confess all he knew. Little time, however, was
given him for the execution of his threats, for on the same
night, at the early hour of nine, he was basely *murdered* in
the streets of Nauvoo. Knocked down with clubs and
stabbed with his *own bowie knife;* he lay reeking in blood,
another victim to the vengeance of the Mormons!

No effort was made by the authorities of Nauvoo to ferret
out and arrest the murderers, and soon after Brigham Young
told his followers, in a public discourse, that " *they had no
business to inquire who killed Erwin Hodge—that no man,
who was a man, would do it, and that every member of the
Church must mind his own business.*"

Hopelessly, entirely now, the prisoners were forced to
submit to their certain fate, and passing the hours within the
lonely confines of their prison cells, watched the sunbeams
as they crept upon the dusty walls, and counted the moments as they passed, hastening them towards the day of
their execution.

CHAPTER. V.

THE ROBBERY OF STRAWN.

THE sentence against Stephen and William Hodges was carried into effect on the 15th of July. They were publicly executed. When on the scaffold they with bold effrontery charged the Court and Jury with injustice in convicting them, as they alleged without sufficient evidence, in the asseverations of innocence, with which many criminals perish upon the scaffold, after a fair trial and conviction, which, perhaps, proves nothing but the natural and universal desire to leave names behind, which at least some one may believe, not wholly linked with infamy. Yet even this consolation must be denied to these unfortunate men. No one doubted their guilt.

The gang finding that all their efforts to save the Hodges had proved unavailing, and believing me to be the prime mover in the events which had led to their arrest and execution, cherished towards me the most bitter and malignant enmity. Not a day passed in which my life was not threatened. I was told that it would not be safe for me to be seen abroad, and that if I showed myself in the streets of Nauvoo, I should have my throat cut, and my body chopped into mince-meat, and that forty men in Nauvoo were ready to carry their threat into execution.

I only mention things of this nature to show the task I had undertaken from a sense of duty to society to perform, was one by no means free from danger; but I ask nothing from the community at large, except a willing belief on their part that I was actuated by honorable motives, and a sincere desire to relieve the country from the depredations of a band of lawless and unprincipled villains. Their threats had no further effect upon me than to induce a stronger determination than ever to ferret out the whole gang, and see justice fully satisfied, as far as the law of the land would admit.

The band of robbers, feeling strong in their united organization, and not intimidated by the breach made in their ranks by the execution of the Hodges, still continued their depredations.

On the night of the 7th of June, 1845, Jeremiah Strawn, an aged man, was quietly reposing after the toils of the day in his house in Putnam County, Illinois. His wife, the partner of his old age as of his youth, was at his side, and in a neighboring room a worthy member of the Methodist Conference was enjoying the rest afforded by the hospitality of the good old couple. It was a lovely night of the most lovely month of the year; and the beholder as he looked out upon that peaceful scene—the quiet farm-house, and the broad level meadows around it, waving their burden of verdure in the pure and holy calm of the moon's soft light—would hardly have thought it possible that beings with the name and capacities of men would dare to mar the sacred serenity of the time and place with deeds of wrong and outrage. It would seem so much like sacrilege before the altar of God's holiest temple of worship.

Near the hour of midnight three men forced their way into that peaceful dwelling and aroused the old man and his wife from their slumbers. One of them with a loaded pistol in his hand approached their bedside, threatening them with instant death if they made the slightest resistance or alarm. Another ruffian stepped to the chamber door, and stood with drawn weapons, ready to prevent any person who might be sleeping in the upper rooms from coming to the assistance of those below, while the third villain, thus protected by his comrades, acted as speaker in the adventure:

"Give us your money!" he said, "or we will kill you both, and set your house on fire!"

"What I have you will find in that bureau yonder," replied Mr. Strawn, who perceived at once the folly of resistance.

"You have more than this!" exclaimed the robber after searching the bureau. "Here are only one hundred dollars in decent money, and about the same in Illinois canal scrip, which is not worth much to us anyway. These two old silver watches are good for little or nothing. We must have more!"

"It is all that I have," said Mr. Strawn, throwing himself back resignedly. "If you kill me you will find no more!"

"Well we won't take your word for it—we'll examine this next room,—who is in here?"

"A Methodist clergyman," replied Mr. Strawn, "he is a poor man, and cannot have much money with him. I hope you will not disturb him."

"Oh! if he is a preacher, we will kill him anyhow," said the robber. "There is no sin in killing a preacher. He will go straight to Heaven, you know! What do you say,

4

boys! shall we put a stop to his sermonizing for the present?"

Thus speaking he entered the room and robbed the affrighted clergyman, who did not seem anxious for an immediate departure to the other world, of his silver watch and about fifteen dollars in money.

" I say, boys," exclaimed the somewhat facetious robber, " if we are caught in this scrape, I reckon we will get off on the plea of insanity, for none but insane persons would think seriously of finding anything worth stealing about a Methodist preacher."

After searching the house from top to bottom, the villains got ready to depart:

" Look here," said one of them, addressing Mr. Strawn," do you intend to follow us?"

" I don't know that I shall."

" You had better not undertake it. You are a dead man if you do. Besides it will do you no good. You can't catch us. So good bye, old fellow."

Early the next morning Mr. Strawn gave the alarm, and with the assistance of his friends, made great exertions to track and apprehend the robbers of his house, but all his efforts were unavailing. Mr. Strawn was left to suffer his misfortunes without remedy.

Not far from the middle of the same month the law office of Knox & Dewey, of Rock Island, Illinois, was broken open and robbed of six hundred and forty dollars, and no trace of the robbers was ever discovered.

About the 25th of the month, an attempt was made to rob Mr. Beach, a merchant in Nauvoo. This robbery was planned by Amos Hodges and R. H. Bleeker, who as security for the Hodges signed the note to Hall & Mills, and Judge Fox, one of their witnesses.

This Amos Hodges was an Elder among the Mormons. Mr. Beach being also a Mormon, the worthy and scrupulous Amos entertained some doubts as to the propriety of robbing his " Brother Beach." Thereupon, as was the custom among the Mormons, upon the eve of any important undertaking, Amos took counsel with Brigham Young.

Whether Brigham favored the proposed robbery or not, is not known, as Amos was forced to seek safety in flight about this time, after being bailed by William Smith and Ripley.

It is certainly in favor of Young that he gave some kind of intimation to Beach of the intended robbery of his premises, thus enabling him with an armed guard to watch the approach of the Banditti.

Fox and Bleeker, accomplished in their hazardous profession, entered the house of Beach with so much silence and skill, that, notwithstanding the careful lookout kept for them, they had nearly succeeded in escaping with a large leathern trunk, which they had taken from the top of a bureau, before they were discovered. This trunk contained between three and four thousand dollars. The guard fired several shots at them, but they escaped without injury, and with no other loss than one of Bleeker's shoes, which was afterwards found in a mud-puddle near the house.

This attempted robbery was ot once made public. Yet no effort was made by Beach or the authorities of Nauvoo to arrest the Banditti.

CHAPTER VI.

THE MURDER OF DAVENPORT.

ON the western shore of Rock Island, looking over the main branch of the Mississippi, and facing Iowa, stands a beautiful residence, adorned by the hand of taste and wealth.

Here many years ago resided Colonel George Davenport. Rock Island had been his home for more than thirty years, and his name was identified with the recollections of the neighborhood, and its history, for a whole generation. He was universally loved and esteemed for his generous heart and social qualities. His wealth had been acquired as an Indian trader, and its acquisition had in no respect stained his honor, for in all his dealings he had been honest and upright. He was an Englishman by birth, but had come to America at an early age. One of the first and true pioneers of the march of civilization in the great northwest, his hold upon the affections of the residents of that part of the territory was strong and abiding.

It was indeed peculiarly mournful that the Banditti of the Prairies, amid their outrages upon society, could not have passed by one so loved and so honored.

It was on the 4th of July, 1845. At the court house in the town of Rock Island, on the main land of Illinois, a large concourse of people assembled, among whom were the family and domestics of Colonel Davenport, to do honor to the glorious birth-day of American Independence. The old man remained at home alone. His family objected to leaving him thus unprotected, for there was a general fear of the Banditti, at that time in all parts of the northwest, between the Rock and Mississippi Rivers. He, however, insisted that all of them should attend the celebration, and disdained the idea that there was any cause whatever for alarm. The venerable old man could not believe that there was danger to him. Safely had he passed through the perils incident to a frontier life—the horrors of Indian warfare, and the dangers of a lonely residence on the very outskirts of civilization, and now that he was surrounded by all the blessings of a peaceful life, and in the midst of a long established community, it is no wonder that the old man could not realize the idea of danger.

This feeling of security frequently accompanies men who have passed through many perils, and it is no uncommon event for such men to perish from carelessness and inattention, which other men would not have practiced. This feeling may have been the true cause of the death of several of our daring soldiers, who, after passing through all the dangers of the Mexican war, have since died when surrounded by all the protections and privileges of peace. Perhaps thus persisted the chivalrous Worth—the gallant Duncan, and the wild and daring Dan Henrie, and other kindred spirits.

" Go," said the old Colonel, with a benevolent smile lighting up his wrinkled face, " Go, my friends, and enjoy yourselves, I feel secure from all harm."

After their departure, he seated himself in his parlor reading his newspaper, or following with a pleased gaze the turbulent motions of the Mississippi, as it rushed by the lovely island of his home. At length his attention was attracted by a faint noise in the vicinity of his well, which did not annoy him as he supposed it was made by some one engaged in drawing water. Presently hearing another noise he arose from his chair to go and ascertain the cause of it, when the door was suddenly pushed open and three men stood before him.

Not a word was said, but almost instantly the foremost of the assassins discharged a pistol at the old man. The ball passed through his left thigh, and as the Colonel turned to grasp his cane, which stood near him, the three men rushed upon him, blindfolded him, pinioned his arms and legs with hickory bark, and dragged him by his long grey hair, cravat and shirt collar into the hall, and up a flight of stairs to a closet, containing an iron safe. This they compelled him to open, being unable from the peculiar structure of the lock to open it themselves. When he had unfastened the private bolt, they took out the contents, and then dragging him into another room, placed him upon a bed, and with terrible threats demanded more money. The old man pointed them with a feeble hand to a drawer in a dressing table near by. The murderers in their hurry missed the drawer containing the money, and opened one in which they found nothing of value. Enraged at their failure, and believing that their defenceless victim intended to deceive them; they flew upon him with violence, and beat and choked him until he passed into a state of insensibility. They then proceeded to recall his senses by dashing water in his face, and when he was restored again demanded money of him; and following the motions of his hand, for he was unable to speak, they again missed the proper drawer. Still more angry, if possible, than at first, they repeated their fiendish brutality upon his person, strangling him until he again fainted. Reviving him by throwing water in his face, and by pouring it down his mouth, they then threatened " to fry him upon coals of fire," if he did not disclose the place where the money had been left, and they would then burn his body in the flames of his own house. The old man fell back insensible, and totally unable to answer them.

The murderers having found between six and seven hundred dollars in money, a gold watch and chain, a double-barrelled shot-gun and pistol, fled precipitately, as if under the influence of some sudden fear, leaving the house sprinkled with blood from parlor to chamber, and the venerable old pioneer, apparently dead upon the bed.

A more cowardly, cold-blooded murder was never committed. The annals of crime have no record which more fully awakens the deepest execrations of the human heart. It seems strange to us that man can ever become so wholly perverted as to take the life of his fellow being. The instinctive shudder with which we shrink back from the slightest idea of destroying the vital principle which animates—a kindred spirit to that which beats within ourselves—the frame work of another, seems a feeling natural and universal. There is not perhaps one among our readers who would not dread to take the life of another, even in self-defence. Yet this old man was murdered in cold blood, within the walls of his own peaceful mansion, and surrounded by the scenes of his long and happy life.

We may not know the after feelings of his murderers, but we cannot but believe that his aged and blood-stained form, like the ghost of the murdered Banquo, must have ever been before their mental vision, a thing of terror and dread.

The first discovery of the murder was made by Mr. Cole of Moline, who with two other men was passing down the Mississippi in a skiff. When nearly opposite the mansion of Colonel Davenport, they heard the cry of murder. Rowing to the shore, they hastened to the house, and on entering the door, which stood ajar, they found blood in every direction, and again heard the fearful cry for help issuing from the chamber. Mr. Cole hurried up stairs where he beheld the terrible spectacle of Colonel Davenport weltering in his blood, and everything around him saturated with his own gore. Mr. Cole, leaving his comrades to render what assistance they might be able to the Colonel, ran for Dr. Brown, who was with a picnic party on the Island, at no great distance from the house; other medical aid was also procured with as much expedition as possible.

Colonel Davenport becoming somewhat restored by the assistance rendered him, was able to tell the circumstances of his murder, and to greet his family upon their return, but being in extreme agony from the torture of the wounds inflicted by the assassins, continued to fail, and finally expired between nine and ten o'clock of the evening after the assault upon him.

After a long and useful life and a terrible death he sleeps well, by the side of the great father of waters, whose waves as they rush to join the ocean, seem to murmur a eulogy and requiem for the good man departed.

His funeral sermon was preached on the following Sunday by the Rev. Mr. Goldsmith of Davenport, from Matthew XII, 39th verse: "*And this know, that if the good man of the house had known what hour the thief would come, he would have watched and not have suffered his house to be broken through.*"

Colonel Davenport described the three assassins who attacked him—one, as being a small, slightly-built man, wearing a cloth cap—one, a short, thick-set, square-built man; and the other, as a large, middling sized, tall man. His description of their features was sufficiently minute to excite suspicion of any person in the neighborhood, and as his aged eyes became closed in death, nothing remained to his family and friends in their earnest desires for justice and vengeance, but to quietly await the events of time, and the mysterious developments of an overruling Providence.

Great exertions were made by the citizens of Rock Island and vicinity to apprehend the murderers. A reward of fifteen hundred dollars was offered by the family of Colonel Davenport for their arrest. Handbills were published, describing the watch and a part of the money, with as minute an account as could be given of the appearance and general character of the three assassins, as described by their victim on his death bed. Companies were organized under the direction of discreet and experienced officers— the country was searched in every direction, and a night watch kept up, but all to no purpose. Day after day the search was continued, but not the slightest information could be obtained of the murderers. The alarm spread far and wide, but the assassins had made good their escape, and the only witness able to identify them, the lamented Colonel Davenport, could give no testimony in an earthly court of justice. His evidence was deferred to be handed in at that great court of last appeal, the judgment tribunal of God; where no witness shall be absent, and no prisoner found wanting, and no victim silenced in death; but face to face, murderer and murdered shall stand, in the clear and blazing ght of the great white throne of the Eternal Judge of all

CHAPTER VII.

PREPARATIONS FOR THE DISCOVERY OF THE MURDERERS.

ON the 8th day of July, the fourth after the murder, while at West Point, Lee County, Iowa, in company with Sheriff Estes, I received intelligence of the murder of Colonel Davenport, of Rock Island, accompanied by a hand-bill describing the appearance of the three men.

I at once suspected, from the description, the persons of John Long and Judge Fox, two of the witnesses for the Hodges, and a man calling himself Blecher, who had assisted Fox in the robbery of Beach, the Nauvoo merchant, a few days previous to the murder of Davenport, my sus-picions also fastened upon him, as the third of the persons referred to by the Colonel.

Sheriff Estes at once addressed a letter to the Sheriff of Rock Island County, recommending him to consult with me as a person well acquainted in Nauvoo, and one employ-ed by the authorities of Lee County, to assist in the discov-ery of Tom Brown, one of the murderers, with the Hodges, of Miller and Liecy.

I also appended a note to the sheriff's letter, stating my own belief as to the guilty persons, describing them from my own recollections, and offering my hearty co-operation in aid of their discovery and apprehension.

On the 15th of July, Hibbard Moore, Esq., called upon me at my residence in Montrose, to whom I gave all the information in my power. He proceeded down the river, as far as Keokuk, but getting no track of the murderers, returned to Rock Island.

In the meantime, by means of my correspondence, I ascertained the names of all the Hodges' witnesses and other information relative to them. I also learned that the two Longs, Fox and Blecher were in the habit of stopping with a man by the name of Old Grant Redden, whose residence was appropriately located near Devil Creek, about five miles from Montrose. I discovered that this Redden kept a general rendezvous for the Banditti. There were four men seen at Redden's about the 8th of July, and had soon after taken their departure for Missouri. I also heard that four or five men of suspicious appearance were lurking about Fort Madison on the 28th and 29th of June, and took passage on the steamboat Osprey for Galena.

At the request of the friends of the late Colonel Davenport, I visited Rock Island on the 21st of July, to give my aid and counsel in devising means to discover the murderers. Of course I found them all extremely anxious to get upon their track. But the whole affair was shrouded in the deepest mystery. A Mr. Bird was arrested on suspicion of being one of the murderers, and committed to the jail at Rock Island, but investigation clearly proved him innocent of the crime. Joseph Knox, Esq., of Rock Island, had in his possession a letter dated 10th of July, from an eminent lawyer of Rockford, Aaron L. Miller, Esq., which he submitted to my perusal. From this letter I discovered that the description of the person who shot Colonel Davenport, resembled the appearance of the notorious Birch, one of the most daring and desperate members of the gang. This Birch was a man of about twenty-five or thirty years of age, and had been suspected of robbery and even of murder, ever since he had attained the age of fifteen years. He was a well-made broad-breasted man, of a light complexion, large blue eyes, and light auburn hair; when fashionably dressed seemed rather slightly built. He was very loqua cious, and could play the bar-room dandy to perfection. Rock Island had been one of his most frequented haunts, where he was known by the name of Brown; he had also appeared in different parts of the country under the names of Birch, Harris and others. After robbing Mr. Mulford, in Winnebago County, he had sought the banks of the Mississippi, as the theatre of his exploits. He was also the chief operator in robbing McKinney and the stage of Frink, Walker & Co., etc., etc. He was undoubtedly one of the most adroit villains in the territory of the northwest.

On the strength of this letter I brought the whole force of my investigation to bear upon this man Birch. My first discovery was, that he was the same man, known at Nauvoo, and already frequently mentioned in the narration, under the name of Blecher. This still confirmed my former opinon relative to the murderers of Colonel Davenport. As yet, however, nothing had been discovered that would warrant their arrest, with any probability of their conviction, unless the money or watch could be found upon them. Being assured of a warm and free support in whatever measures I might choose to adopt for the discovery of the murderers, I consented, after much persuasion, to devote my time and efforts to the undertaking. I was therefore

continually at work collecting information, and also in
securing such legal documents as might be necessary for the
arrest of suspected persons.

On my return home from Rock Island sickness in my
family compelled me to suspend all active exertion for a
time, but I kept a watchful eye upon the movements of the
gang in my immediate vicinity, and thought upon various
schemes to get track of the murderers. Some of the friends
of the gang suspecting my design, and, with the intention
of misleading me, told me that the watch taken from
Colonel Davenport, was then in the possession of one of the
Banditti, by the name of Millard, who was then near
Galena, and that the murderers themselves were on the
Illinois river; with many other equally false reports.

About this time, the citizens of Montrose became exas-
perated beyond endurance at the repeated and almost daily
larcenies committed in their neighborhood, and some stolen
property being traced to the house of a man by the name of
Potter, living on the bank of the Mississippi, half a mile
above the town, and who kept a ferry known as Thier
Ferry, for the accommodation of the Nauvoo portion of the
gang, determined to check the operations of the band of
thieves, by what appeared to be the only remedy.

Some twenty or thirty of the citizens collecting together,
proceeded to the house of Potter, and removing all the
furniture from the house, laid the dwelling level with the
ground.

Potter, breathing vengeance, removed his effects to Nauvoo, and took up his residence with the most noted members
of the gang. The citizens then determined to make a
similar ejectment of Old Redder from Devil's Creek. I
however earnestly remonstrated against this attempt, and

after much persuasion induced them to abandon it. I showed them that an interference with the Reddens at this time might be the means of counteracting all my plans relative to ferreting out the murderers of Davenport.

At length, my suspicions of the assassins were fully corroborated. A certain John Baker, one of the gang, came into Montrose, soon after the destruction of Potter's house, with a splendid span of bay horses which he offered for sale. I took occasion to converse with Baker frequently, and partially gained his confidence. After many allusions to the various operations of the Banditti, in a manner calculated to carry the idea to him that I was in fact "one of the b'hoys," I at length ventured to mention the name of the Longs, and Fox, with others of the gang.

" Ah!" said he, " you are acquainted with Fox?"

" Well acquainted with all of them," was the reply.

" Where are the boys now ? "

I don't know exactly. I have not seen them for some time."

" I have not seen Fox and the Longs in several months," said Baker, " since last winter I have been in the upper part of Missouri, and have not known much of what was going on along the river."

" Are you acquainted with the Reddens?"

" Only by reputation. I have frequently heard the boys speak of them."

" I think you might learn where some of our fellows are, by going to old man Redden's. They usually stop with him when in this vicinity; he lives only four or five miles distant."

" I would like to see some of them," said Baker, " I used to travel with them, but Fox and I have had a little difficulty

about some property we once owned in company, so I
concluded to sparate—let them go to the devil their
own way, and I will go mine."

"What property was it?"

"Oh! some goods we had up on the Sharridon river.
Fox went south to spend the winter, while I staid
behind to sell the goods.   When he returned, he insisted that I did not account for all I had sold.   I would
not stand this, so we dissolved partnership, and since
then I have not had much deal with him.   Yet I would
like to see some of the old fellows."

"Then you had better get on a horse and ride out to
Redden's.   It will take you but a short time.   If you
go, you need not mention my name, as 1 am not per-
sonally acquainted with the old man, and he might
think something was wrong."

"I won't—never fear.   I know how to satisfy him
that I am all right."

Saying this, Baker left me, and soon after started
for Devil Creek.   After being gone nearly a day, he
returned.   I asked him what luck he had had.

"First rate," he replied.

"Did you see any of the boys?"

"No, but I heard all about them."

"What did you hear?"

"Why, d—n it, man," he said in a low whisper
"they are the ones who killed old Col. Davenport."

"Is it so?   How do you know that?"

"*Old Redden* told me all about it."

"He did?   I should have thought he would have
kept close about that."

" When I first got there, the old man was a little afraid of me, but I told him who I was, and he recollected hearing the boys speak of me. So, becoming satisfied that I was one of the *right stripe*, he told me the whole story."

" Well," replied I, " keep a tight mouth about it, or the boys will get into trouble. What is the old man's history of the affair? "

" Fox, John, Aaron, and Birch started from Old Redden's to rob the Colonel, and when they returned with their booty, they buried the watch and money in the old fellow's wheat field. They staid there until they received information that Davenport was dead, when they put off."

" Where are they now? "

" They went back into Missouri, but Old Redden does not know exactly where they are at this time."

" They are safe, anyway, I suppose."

" Oh, yes! they are acquainted all through the country, and have got lots of friends."

" How did they hear that the old Colonel was dead? "

" Aaron Long and Harrison Redden went over to Nauvoo, and while there saw a handbill describing three of them, the watch, and part of the money. They returned to Old Redden's, told the news to John, Fox, and Birch, and they all left the same night."

This intelligence connected with circumstances previously brought to light, fully confirmed in my own mind, the guilt of the two Longs, Fox, and Birch. Also the guilt of the Reddens as accessories. Still there was not a particle of direct evidence, and much remained to be done.

Sheriff Estes and James Knox, Esq., were informed of the facts elicited by my conversation with Baker, but the same was necessarily kept from the public.

5

A ray of hope had at length dawned upon us. We were
satisfied that we knew who the murderers were. The task
which remained was to discover the evidence necessary to
convict them. It is a beautiful feature of the great system
of law, that the clearest and most undoubted evidence is
always required in order to convict the criminal, and the
fact that the ends of justice are sometimes defeated by this
strict requisition does not at all militate against its equity as
a fixed and abstract rule of action.

On the 1st of August I received a letter from Mr.
Samuel Fisher of Rock Island, in which he spoke of information obtained by Mr. Knox, relative to that portion of the
Banditti who infested the country in and around Dixon.
Developments had been made by a late member of the gang
named West, by which it was ascertained that this same
Robert H. Birch was their acknowledged leader, and
generally known among them by the name of " The Captain," though often assuming the aliases above spoken of:
Bob Harris, Haines, Brown, Blecher, etc. The description
of him in this letter accords fully with the one already
given. He frequently made a temporary abiding place at
the residence of a man by the name of Bennet, in Iowa, four
miles above Lyons, on the Mississippi river.

This letter also gave a minute description of James
Veasey, John Killgore, alias Big Davis, William Sutton,
(whose real name was William Fox,) and stated that
Governor Ford of Illinois had offered a reward of two hundred dollars for the apprehension of each person concerned
in the murder of Colonel Davenport.

I continued my search in Nauvoo and its vicinity,
obtaining additional items of importance, until the 7th of
August, when I received a letter by the hands of Mr.

Fisher, which it may not be uninteresting to give verbatim, as showing the deep feeling of the community in relation to the horrid murder:

ROCK ISLAND, Aug. 6, 1845.

DEAR SIR: Mr. Fisher starts for your place to-day with a view to render you any and all the aid he can in ferreting out the murderers. Our anxiety for the speedy arrest of these wretches is so great, that we feel inclined to sacrifice time, money, comfort, anything and everything, to effect the object.

We cluster all our hopes around your plans and efforts. Don't let us be disappointed. Heaven send you prosperity and success. With much esteem,

Yours truly,

JOSEPH KNOX.

With those who had watched the movements of the gang, and carefully noted the intelligence received from different sources up to the present time, not a shadow of doubt remained as to the guilt of Fox, Birch and the two Longs. How many more were concerned as accessories, it was impossible to imagine. All who were in possession of this information were eager for the pursuit and arrest of the villains.

Yet as far as I had investigated the circumstances, I was unable to point even to one item of testimony that would legally prove their guilt before a court and jury. The description given by Col. Davenport of itself could avail nothing. The fact of their participating in other crimes had nothing to do with the case now under consideration, and any indirect information drawn from members of the gang, could not of course be brought into use as competent evidence. I confess, that confident as I was in my knowledge of the guilty persons, I felt much disheartened in view of the present aspect of the case. The idea of attempting to pursue and arrest four desperate robbers and murderers, who were constantly committing their deeds of darkness, and escaping from point to point under cover of the night, and changing their names with every change of the wind, with no other track than the one left in their flight from Old Redden's, and that already one month old, certainly gave little prospect of success. I felt most heartily willing to aid the authorities of Rock Island to the extent of my ability, yet to assume the responsibility of conducting an enterprise of this magnitude was a task I could not willingly undertake. The threats made by the Banditti against me individually, in consequence of the part I had already taken in the arrest and prosecution of the Hodges, convinced me that some danger must attend the undertaking.

After careful thought and reflection, however, I came to the decision, that the duty which I owed to my fellows, as one of the members of the great social compact, was superior to all other considerations, and this determination being once adopted, my after course of action was pursued without fear or hesitation.

On the 11th of August I again visited Rock Island, and held a consultation with some of the prominent citizens of the place and neighborhood.

In this consultation the subject was viewed in two lights. We must either abandon all hopes of bringing the murderers to justice, submit quietly to the ravages of the Banditti, and suffer ourselves, our friends and our neighbors, to share the fate of Miller, Liecy, and Davenport, or, on the other hand, the most earnest and determined effort must be made to rescue the distracted country from the ruthless ravages of this organized band.

It was finally decided that some person should be selected whose duty it should be to adopt some plan to get admitted as one of the members of the gang; obtain their full confidence, and by searching out, and connecting facts, eventually secure the arrest and conviction of the guilty wretches.

I was earnestly solicited to undertake this dangerous adventure. I declined, and plead my situation in excuse. I had a wife and children, and failure in the attempt was certain death. But no other person could be found who was considered competent to the task, and the visage of the venerable and lamented Davenport—his gray hairs clotted with blood, and his frame distorted in the agonies of a terrible death, cried aloud for vengeance and justice.

I at length consented, expecting and receiving a pledge for the support and protection of my family and the education of my children, in the event of my losing my life in the adventure.

I obtained the necessary legal documents from the authorities of Rock Island County, and prepared to proceed to Galena and the mining regions of Wisconsin and Iowa, with letters to Hons. Judge Brown, J. P. Hoge, Judge Wilson, and General Wilson, citizens of Galena and Dubuque. In these letters the secret and hazardous nature of my business was fully set forth, and their co-operation solicited, which I need not say was readily accorded.

At Dubuque, his Honor Judge Wilson accompanied me to the Miner's Bank, and aided me in obtaining blank sheets of bank notes, by the possession of which I hoped to decoy the gang into full confidence.

At the risk of being considered somewhat too minute, I shall proceed to narrate my endeavors to get admission to the ranks of the Banditti, in some of which I was on the wrong track, or at least not in the most direct one.

CHAPTER VIII.

THE day following my visit to the Miners' Bank at Dubuque, I returned to Galena and made vigilant search for the man said to have possession of Col. Davenport's watch. At length I found a man that I believed to be the person.

Addressing him without introduction, and with the freedom which the frankness and cordiality of Western life and social intercourse justifies, after some preliminary and unimportant conversation, I said:

"Sir, I have your name from a source which I think entitles me to approach you in a confidential manner. Have you a private room at the hotel?"

"Yes! follow me," he said, conducting me to his apartment.

"Look at these articles," said I, drawing the bank bills from my pocket, and presenting them for his inspection, "What do you think of them?"

After a long and critical examination, he replied:

"They are very good, but I think the paper is a little thinner than that issued by the bank."

"Not much," was my answer; "they may appear thin now, but by use, you know, they will collect dirt, and become rough, when they will seem about as thick as the genuine note paper."

" They are the best I ever saw in this country; but we are too near the bank for a successful disposition of them. Being rather thin, they would soon be detected. It is only fifteen miles from here to the Dubuque Bank."

" I know it is not far," I said, " yet I believe we might put a few thousand of these bills in circulation around Galena, without detection."

" Perhaps so. I acknowledge it is a strong temptation, but I do not want to touch the matter. Let me tell you, sir, I am now doing a good, honest business—no matter what I have done. I have had nothing to do with matters of this kind since I left Detroit. If I should be suspected it would injure me more than all I could make out of it. But there are enough others who would be glad to get as good an article as this."

" I know that well enough."

" How much of it have you?"

" About fifteen thousand dollars."

" A good operation ought to be made out of that amount."

" Yes. Are you acquainted in this part of the country?"

" I am generally acquainted in this vicinity."

" Do you know the name of Long or Fox?"

" No, not any by those names."

" If I could find them, I think we could come to an understanding very soon."

" The only man in this part of the country I am acquainted with who deals in matters of this kind, lives three or four miles east of here. You had better go and see him. A any rate, I won't have anything to do with it."

I had become convinced that this man had no connection whatever with the Banditti, and was not the one described as having possession of Col. Davenport's watch. Although it is probable, that at some period of his life, he had been engaged in criminal transactions, yet, as he had manifested a desire to abandon them, and lead an honorable life, I will not mention his name. It is very difficult to return to the path of virtue, after having wandered in the by-ways of vice, and when any one attempts it, all should be cautious how they throw impediments in the way.

I, however, called upon the man he referred me to, but got no intelligence whatever from him.

After spending several days among the lead mines, and becoming satisfied that the story of the watch being in that neighborhood was a ruse intended to mislead me, I took passage on board the steamboat War Eagle, bound for St. Louis.

Soon after leaving the port, a young man addressed me by my name. I did not at first remember him.

" My name is Young," he said, " I was sick last winter in Loomis' tavern at Nauvoo, and saw you occasionally in the bar-room. I finally remembered hearing of him, as one of the gang, at the time of my search after Tom Brown.

" Seeing that we are old acquaintances, Mr. Young," I said " suppose we go into the saloon and take a social glass!"

" Agreed," he said.

" What kind of speculation are you in now-a-days? " I asked as we touched glasses. "

" Nothing in particular. I have been at work of late a few miles from Galena. A while ago, I was up as far as Prairie du Chien, on a little operation."

" I think I am not mistaken," said I, " in taking you for one of the *right stripe?* "

" Well, I don't know! What do you call the *right stripe?* "

" Pshaw. you know what I mean."

A half smile played around his lips as he replied:

" Oh, if you mean a fellow that likes a glass now and then, I am of the right stripe—let's take another!"

I found this man constantly on his guard, and returning with him to the hurricane deck, after much conversation in which I aimed to draw from him some account of the operations of the gang, I was obliged to give him up for a bad job, as far as the present time was concerned.

Early the next morning I again met Young in the saloon, and walking to the hurricane deck, I accosted him with the remark, that I had heard his name mentioned as one of our sort of boys, "and," continued I, " if you will promise me the most profound secresy, I would like to show you a little matter that is worth looking at."

" I promise," he said.

" Look at these blank bills on the Miners' Bank at Dubuque, and see if you could tell them from the genuine."

After a very close inspection, he remarked,

"That's a d——d good article: how much of it have you got?"

" Only enough for a sample, with me."

" How much can you raise like it?"

" About fifteen thousand dollars. I must, however, go to Cincinnati first, as none of it as yet is filled up or signed."

" It is really a splendid imitation. How much do you ask per dollar for it?"

" I don't know exactly, 'until I count up all of the ex-
penses connected with preparing it."

" It is worth the highest price!"

" How much do you usually pay for this kind of article?"

" We pay from fifteen to twenty-five dollars a hundred.
When it is new, if good, like this, it is worth about twenty-
five per cent. After it it detected, and *blown* in the news-
papers, of course it is not worth so much."

" No, certainly not."

" I'll give you twenty-five per cent for this, and find a
market for all you have or can raise."

" I don't think I can afford it for twenty-five dollars on a
hundred. It has cost me a pile of money to get it up, and
it is about as good as the genuine bills right out of the
bank."

" True, it is."

" I think I ought to have half the face of it, but if I can
make sale of all I have, I will let it go for something less.
I shall, however, insist upon the best kind of funds, if I
sell it for anything short of fifty per cent."

" That is fair enongh," said he, still continuing to gaze
upon the money with undisguised admiration.

"Besides it will take one some time to go to Cincinnati,
and get it all signed, and return with it."

" That will just suit me, for my pockets are pretty light
now. I'm nearly *strapped.* I shall make a raise pretty
soon, however, and I know lots of the boys who will buy
it."

" You ought not to get dead broke, when you have
nothing to do but to rake down some man, and there are
plenty of them in this part of the country who have got
money."

"It is not so easy making a raise, when one is broke; half the sights we undertake are failures. Then we have a good many to divide with, and it costs fellows of our free and easy habits something to live."

"Yes, so it does."

"When I have money, I always spend it freely."

"That's the only way to live."

"As far as I am concerned, I would not live any other,"

"But you occasionally *raise* a horse, and make something that way, do you not?"

"Yes, that was my operation at Prairie du Chien; I took two good horses up there, but sold them cheap, and have been spreeing it ever since."

"Are you entirely out of money?"

"I haven't got enough to pay my fare on the boat, but I shall raise some at Nauvoo. I have lots of friends in that place."

"Let me lend you a few dollars," said I, handing them to him. "You can repay me at some convenient time."

"Thank you, I can go through on this."

"I never allow any of the right stripe to want for money when I have plenty myself."

"You are a d——d good, whole-souled fellow. I was a little afraid of you at first."

"No more than was proper. We must all be careful. I suppose the boys about Nauvoo have plenty of money now. They have made some pretty good *hauls* of late."

"Yes, I reckon they have. I have not been in Nauvoo since spring. I shall stop there now."

"Do you know Jack Redden of Devil Creek?"

"Very well."

"What do you think of him?"

"I don't like him. He is not honorable among his friends."

"Is he not? I thought he was true blue."

"I have been in a good many *snaps* with Jack. He always manages to get the money into his own hands, and holds on to it, like the cholera to a nigger. I know of several good sights which I intend to raise as soon as I can get the right kind of boys to help me, but Jack Redden can't have a chance in; he has cheated me enough already."

"Were it not that I must go to Cincinnati immediately, I would like to go in with you."

"I would like to have you."

"How many would be necessary to *raise the sights?*"

"Three or four would be enough."

"Where are they?"

"Two at Dubuque, one in Iowa nearly opposite the mouth of the Fever River, and three or four a few miles from Galena in the lead mines."

"Why did you not raise them when you were up there?"

"The boys up around Galena are d—d cowards. They dare not do anything. There is Millard who keeps a grocery about two miles east of Galena. He is a great braggart, but dare not do anything without some of us go ahead; and then he is as leaky as an old boat, always telling everything. I dare not have anything to do with him. Then there is Aaron Long, but he won't do anything without the Judge."

"Ah!" thinks I to myself, "thank heaven, I am getting him into the true track at last."

"So, you see," continued he, "the boys are all lying on their oars. I wouldn't give a d—n for such partners."

"Who do you mean by the Judge?"

" You must know him!"

" The boys go by so many different names that it is possible I may know him under some other title."

" His name is Fox, and we all look upon him as one of our leaders."

" Can you get Fox to help you make those raises about Galena and Dubuque, by the time that I return from Cincinnati, with these fifteen thousand dollars in Dubuque paper? "

" I am afraid he has left this part of the country, and will not return until fall. Then he will be in Galena, and the boys won't do much until he *does* return."

" If Fox does not return in time, can't we pursuade Aaron Long to help us? I do not see why we should all wait for Fox."

" Aaron told me that he should stay at his father's, out six miles from Galena, until the Judge and John Long come back. Besides, I and Aaron are not good friends. He was dead broke a while ago and I lent him twenty dollars, which he won't pay me now, and he has made a good raise since, too. In fact, the reason I am out of money now is that he won't do the fair thing by me."

" Does *Old Long* understand all the boys' operations?"

" Yes, and the old woman, too."

" Does she? "

" Yes! she is keener than all the rest of the family put together."

" Do John Long and the Judge travel together?"

" Yes, they have done so for the last three or four years, and shared equally in all they could raise."

" I think we had better get some of the boys from Nauvoo, to help us *raise your sights.* I believe Jack Redden can be made to divide honorably."

" Well, I don't. He is not to be trusted. Just let me tell you one of his d———d mean operations."

" A while ago I took a trip with him and William Louther, over on the Illinois River. Louther parted from us at Pekin and ascended the river to look up some sights. Jack Redden and I stopped there with an old Momon, and staid several days While there, Jack preached several times in the neighborhood—pretty fair sermons, too, as well as I can judge of such articles. They all seem to have about the same quantity of fire and brimstone in them, as though men were to be frightened into heaven, rather than reasoned there. Jack put in the big licks, till he made some of them look blue.

" Well, we found the old man had lots of money in the house, and thought it would be charitable to relieve him of some of it. So Jack fixed up a story and told the old Mormon, that Brigham Young wanted to get specie, to purchase materials for the Holy Temple, that could not be obtained for any thing but gold and silver.

" The old Mormon expressed his willingness to make the exchange of specie for bills if it would accommodate Brigham, and gave Jack the gold for a hundred dollar counterfeit bill. A good load—that of Jack's! was'n't it?"

" The old Mormon had sixteen or seventeen hundred dollars in specie left, and we noticed particularly in what part of the house he kept it, and made an agreement with each other to go back and *raise* it.

" When Louther returned, we all started off up the river, and made an easy raise of about two hundred and forty dollars. I did most of this thing myself. I crawled in at a window, over a bed where two persons were sleeping. While getting in, I accidentally put my hand on a person's face, where two persons were sleeping in one bed. Neither of them, however, awoke, and I crept on to a desk containing the money, appropriated it as quietly as possible, and escaped by the same window; making off without waking any one in the house. After this adventure, Jack proposed that we should part for a few days, and appoint a place for meeting. Suspecting nothing, we agreed, and the rascal, the next night went back to the old Mormon's alone, and entering the house, took all his gold, and an hundred dollar counterfeit bill which he had passed upon him, and made off with it without being discovered. He then went and buried it, and would not divide with us. All I got was a third of the two hundred and forty dollars, and such is the way Jack Redden always serves his comrades. I have determined to have no more to do with him."

" Well, he is a shrewd fellow."

" Yes, too d—d shrewd for me."

" Are you acquainted with the old man Redden, and William H. Redden?"

"Oh, yes! I always stop with them. Redden is a fine old fellow. He always keeps the boys when they want to stop with him; and lets them pay up when they are a mind to. Harrison lives at home with the old man, and don't travel much. He is more honorable in his deal with the boys than Jack is."

" I suppose the old man and Harrison know all about your business?"

" Yes, they understand all that is going on. After stopping a few days at Nauvoo, I shall go over to the old man's and stay several weeks."

" Will the Judge and the Longs like to get some of my Dubuque paper?"

" Yes, they will take lots of it."

" Will they *raise* much money this summer?"

" They have made some pretty good raises recently."

" I suppose they *raise* some good horses?"

" Yes, and they look up some first-rate sights!"

" Some of the boys made a good *raise* lately from Col. onel Davenport.   They were smart enough not to get caught.   I have no idea myself who they were."

" Oh! I know all about that."

" Who were they?"

" Judge Fox, Birch, John Long and Aaron Long are the ones who robbed Col. Davenport."

" I was told that Davenport, in his description, spoke only of three men."

" Very true! those were all he saw—but Aaron stood sentry outside, while Fox, John and Birch did the work in the house."

" How much did they get?"

" I saw Aaron, but he would not tell me *how much* they got.   He tried to make me think they got only a small sum, but I knew better.   I saw him have a large roll of Missouri bills, and some silver, and tried to have him pay me that twenty dollars he owed me, but he refused."

" Did you know anything of the Davenport matter, before Aaron told you?"

" Yes, I will tell you all about it.   I had been out on the Illinois river, and raised two horses near Hennepin, I run them across the country to Fort Madison, where I met the Longs, Birch and Fox.   I had not seen them for several months, and inquired what they were doing.   They said they were going up to Rock Island to *rake down* an old man.   I asked them if they had a good sight.   They said that they had, and expected to raise thirty or forty thousand dollars. I proposed to go in with them for the sight, but they refused, saying that their company was made up, and that four was enough to make the raise. I insisted on going in, as I had been with them in a good many hard scrapes, in which we had made little or nothing. But they would not admit me; stating that they had already been at a good deal of expense, and would be obliged to divide with the man who had got up the sight for them. I left them and went out to Devil Creek to rest my horses for a few days— then run up to Prairie du Chien; sold my horses, and returned to old man Long's where I have been staying until I started on this trip down the river."

"Have you seen the boys since you left them at Fort Madison?"

"None but Aaron, he was at his father's when I arrived there from Prairie du Chien."

"Does old Long do anything at this business?"

"Not much. He only keeps a station, and takes care of what the boys bring to him to deposit."

"Did Aaron tell you where the boys met after robbing the old Colonel?"

"They all left the island together, and went down the river to Old Redden's, where they staid until news reached them that Davenport was dead, when Aaron returned home to his father's, and Fox, John and Birch went back into Missouri.

"Well, I suppose they will know enough to take care of themselves and not get caught."

"No danger of that. They are old hands at the business; know how to take care of themselves, and have plenty of friends."

6

Through this long conversation, Young naa made his statements without seeming to have any suspicion; and I determined to keep him talking, as his information was already very valuable, and more yet might be obtained from him.

"Have you made any *raises* since you sold your horses at Prairie du Chien?"

"No; I tried a small one when I reached Dubuque, but did not succeed. I was lounging in a store, and seeing the merchant changing some money, noticed a quantity of gold in his desk. I accordingly watched the store, and while he was at supper, entered the back door, and approached the desk, when, hearing him upon the front steps, I ran out as he was opening the door, and escaped unnoticed."

"After watching for several days, I got in again, and was in the very act of opening the desk, when the merchant entered at the front door. This was just at the dusk of evening. I left very suddenly, as you may imagine, with the merchant at my heels, crying 'stop thief, stop thief,' at the top of his lungs. I ran through the alley, and towards the river, with all possible expedition.

"Near the bank of the river was a house kept by some girls of the right sort, with whom I was well acquainted. When I burst into the house, the merchant was but a few steps behind me. I cried to the girls to hide me."

"Here," said big Maria, "squat in the corner of the room," and she threw some bed clothes over me.

"Where is the thief," cried the merchant, entering the room, the next instant, puffing and blowing like a porpoise.

"Who do you mean?" asked Big Maria, very innocently.

"Did not a man just come in here?"

"Yes, but he passed out at the back door."

" Oh! I'm after him then," and away he went, snuffing
and wheezing like a locomotive, and I saw no more of him.
I tell you, friend! there is nothing like a woman, to keep
a man out of a scrape. She is quicker-witted than a man,
and has more self-command in a tight place. The first
raise I make I shall remember Big Maria—my word for
that. I staid with the girls till about nine o'clock, and then
left town for Galena, and old man Long's."

" How," I asked, " did the boys first learn that Col.
Davenport had money, and by what means they could get
it ?"

" The man who got up the sight lives in the vicinity of
Rock Island, and is quite well acquainted with the
family of Col. Davenport. He has lived with him, worked
for him, and knows all about the situation of the house.
About two weeks before the boys made the raise he went
to Davenport's house, spent the afternoon, and took supper
with the family, under pretence of a friendly visit, but for
the real purpose of ascertaining the situation of the family
at the time, to enable the boys to decide upon the most
practicable mode of attack.

" He ascertained that there were four men in the family
at the time, that they all slept in the upper room, and were
well supplied with weapons of defence, and that the old
man kept his money in a chamber."

" Did you learn the name of this man who got up the
sight?"

" No; in relating the circumstances the boys did not
mention his name."

" Do you think they have gone so far into Missouri that
they will not return by the time I get back from Cincinnati
with the $15,000 of Dubuque paper? I really want to go in
with you to *raise the sights* you speak of."

" They will go to St. Louis, and probably to Indiana, before they return, and will not be in this part of the country before next fall."

" As soon as I get back with this *bogus*, and supply you and your friends, if there is no better speculation on hand I want to take an extensive trip through the country."

" You would have a great time."

" I suppose you are acquainted with all the boys, and can tell me where to go, and who to call upon that are of the *right stripe?*"

" Yes, I know all the boys south and west, as well as those about the lead-mines. I can give you four hundred names if you want them, but you won't need so many."

" Oh, no."

" Tell me which way you want to travel, and I will give you a few names to call on, and those I introduce you to, can give you all the names you will want in travelling from point to point."

" I intend to journey through Missouri to St. Louis; and perhaps travel east or south from that city."

" If you leave the Mississippi and travel west, call on *Packard*, at Packard's Grove, on the Sharridon River, near the line between Missouri and Iowa, about one hundred miles west of the Mississippi River. He keeps a station there, and knows all the boys in the upper part of Missouri. Fox always puts up with him when he travels in that part of the country.

" In St. Louis, find *Thomas Reynolds* who keeps a livery stable, near the corner of Third and Plume Streets. A good many of our fellows stop with him, and he buys horses of them. He is an honorable man, and knows all the boys about St Louis. I know him well; just tell him I told you to call on him, and that will be sufficient introduction.

" On the road leading from St. Louis to St. Charles, about five miles from the city, you will find a man by the name of *Raymond.*

John Birch, father of the Birch who was with Fox and the Longs, when they robbed old Davenport, lives nine miles south-west of Marshall, the county seat of Clark County, Illinois. He keeps a station, and knows all the boys in that vicinity. For a few more of the best kind of fellows I refer you to *John Stow* in Vandalia, Illinois; *Hiram Long,* cousin to John and Aaron Long; *Shock Phips,* and *John Singleton,* all living in the same town, in Owen County, Indiana, south-east of Terre Haute, near Eel River; *Jack Burton,* in Spice Valley, Indiana, and *E. B. Logan,* in Memphis, Tennessee."

" You can call on any of those men. They are all true blue, and of the *right stripe.* They will give you all the information, and render you all the assistance you will need, if you will just tell them that you are a friend of *Granville Young.*"

Thus ended the precious revelations of this rascal. I trust the reader will not consider my long conversation with him devoid of interest. He will perceive that it was of great importance to me in my arduous undertaking; containing a full and explicit statement of the steps of the murderers, previous to the attack upon the mansion of the lamented Davenport.

It also proved that more than Fox, Birch, and the Longs were engaged in that cowardly murder, involving himself as accessory, and placing me upon the track of a new, and perhaps greater scoundrel, than either of those actually engaged in the murder; I mean the villain, who under the guise of friendship, had obtained the necessary information for them, and who was plotting it, even when sharing the hospitality and kindness of the venerable old man, beneath the shadow of his own roof.

CHAPTER IX.

DETENTION of the steamer at Rock Island, enabled me to disclose to those who were in possession of my sceret purpose, the important communications received from Granville Young, and to make further arrangements to prosecute the search for the three murderers who left Redden's for Missouri.

When I had narrated the particulars of the part acted by the man who had visited at the house of Col. Davenport, under the garb of friendship, George L. Davenport, Esq., recognised, in the description, the person of one John Baxter, who had been for several years, and was, at the time of the murder, a resident of Rock Island, but soon after that event had removed to Jefferson, Wisconsin, wholly unsuspected.

This scoundrel, John Baxter, whose name should be printed upon his front, in letters as black as his heart, was now a prominent object of attention, and we rejoiced that, in the event of his conviction, his punishment, as accessory, would be no less severe than that of the active perpetrators of the murder.

As the reader will notice, the present position of the murderers, as far as we had discovered who they were, was as follows: three of the principals, according to the intelligence received by Granville Young, were travelling in the gang. Aaron Long, the other of the murderers, was at his father's, six miles east of Galena. John Baxter was in Jefferson, Wisconsin. Old Grant Redden and Wm. Redden, on Devil Creek, in Lee County, Iowa, and Granville Young was then a passenger on the steamboat, on his way to Nauvoo, and Devil Creek. Most of these could be arrested at our pleasure, but it was determined to suffer the five to remain unmolested, and pursue Fox, John Long and Birch. This must be accomplished by following the trail marked out by Granville Young.

Fearing that the Dubuque blank bills, which had succeeded in winning the confidence of Young, might not be available in all parts of the country through which I must necessarily travel, I made arrangements, by the aid of Joseph Knox, Esq., and others, before leaving Rock Island, to obtain from the State Bank of Missouri, at St. Louis, such blank bills, and other accommodations as I might desire, to decoy the gang, and aid me in the pursuit of the murderers.

Everything being satisfactorily arranged, and the most profound secrecy enjoined upon all concerned in the plot, I left Rock Island upon my downward trip to St. Louis.

Resuming my interview with Young, I obtained much additional information relative to the extensive organization and operations of the gang.

This Young informed me that he was a native of Virginia, and had been a member of the united Banditti for about seven years. He had left his native place about five years before my acquaintance with him commenced, with several stolen horses. Although vigorously pursued, he evaded his followers, and escaped with the horses into Kentucky; then crossing the Ohio River into Indiana, he disposed of his horses without suspicion.

He also stated that *Killgore*, alias Big Davis, who, with Birch and others, robbed Mulford, in Winnebago County, was then on Sherridon River, in the neighborhood of Packard's Grove.

Granville Young left the War Eagle at Nauvoo, from whence he proceeded to Old Redden's on Devil Creek, where he was afterwards arrested.

On arriving at Montrose, I informed James Knox, Esq., of the present abiding place of Killgore, the notorious robber, suggesting that he might be arrested without difficulty.

I also discovered, by conversing with Mr. Loomis, of Nauvoo, that the *bloody coats* found near the Robbers' Camp—so called—he thought he could indentify as being the coats of John Long and Fox. He also believed the gloves belonged to Birch.

This Robbers' Camp was found in the bluffs, south of Rock Island, and near it were discovered two coats stained with blood, concealed under leaves and rubbish. In a pocket of the coat were a pair of kid gloves, afterwards identified as the property of Birch.

On the 23d of August I arrived at St. Louis. I found that notwithstanding the supposed secresy with which our plot was progressing, there was a leaky vessel some where among us, and that some inkling of our project had been seized upon by the editor of the Quincy Whig; in the last number of whose paper an article had appeared containing enough to put the murderers upon their guard. As this article had been copied into the St. Louis papers, my first undertaking was to have it contradicted, in which I succeeded by the aid of Dr. Knox. I felt very much vexed and disheartened at the discovery that some one or more of those in the secret had thus failed to exercise common prudence and caution in a matter of so much importance. I was almost inclined to return home, and abandon all hopes of arresting the perpetrators of the murder. I had attempted an enterprise, hazardous in the extreme—one in which a hope of pecuniary reward alone would never have induced me to engage in, and I certainly was excusable in feeling some discouragement at these premature developments. It would have been time enough to have given facts to the public when it could have been done without prejudice to the public good.

I completed the arrangement with the State Bank of Missouri, and obtained the blank bills agreeably to my request.

While in St. Louis, Dr. Reuben Knox, and J. S. Dougherty, City Marshal, rendered me all the assistance in their power, towards accomplishing the object of my mission.

I inquired for Reynolds, livery stable keeper, to whom I had been referred by Young. His general character, as far as known, the Marshal informed me was good. I determined, however, to give him a call. I met him in the street, and introduced myself as Mr. Brown.

"I have been referred to you Mr. Reynolds, as a gentleman with whom it would be beneficial for me to have a little private conversation."

"Who referred you to me?"

"Granville Young."

"I don't know any such man."

"Do you not?"

"No."

"Do you know Thomas Brown of Nauvoo?"

" No."

" Do you know any one by the name of Long or Birch?"

" No, I do not."

" You are probably then, not the person I was referred to by my friend, Granville Young."

" Where do you reside?" he asked.

" In no particular place. Wherever business calls me."

Reynolds watched the expression of my countenance very closely, and finally said—

" I think I understand your business."

" That is sufficient. The public street is no place for confidential conversation."

" I have no private room."

" Is there no place in which we can meet?"

" Anywhere you please."

" Well, I will get a horse and carriage at the Walton House and we will ride into the country."

" Very well! I will meet you at the Walton House in one hour from this time."

Reynolds met me punctually at the time of his appointment. We rode through the principal streets, and were quite out of the city before I again introduced my business.

" You may think, Mr. Reynolds!" I said, " that I am rather free for a stranger, but when I have satisfactory references, I am not backward in making business known, and have no fears that you will betray me."

" I am not apt to betray confidence."

"Well, then, I will show you a little specimen of work, which I think will meet your approbation. What do you think of it?"

I produced my blank bills on the Miners' Bank and the State Bank of Missouri. After inspecting them he replied—

"It is very good. How much have you like it?"

" Only a few samples, but will soon have plenty of it. When I return I would like to leave a few thousand in the city. Young tells me you are acquainted with all the boys in this vicinity, and would not hesitate to assist me."

" I think I can render you some aid, if you request it. When I first met you, I thought best to be a little careful. It is squally times about here now. The officers are watching for Tinker from Cincinnati, and some others, but they won't find them I reckon."

" Is Tinker in this city?"

·" Yes, but he can't be seen at present."

" Are the boys doing anything in this part of the country now?"

" Not much. I am well acquainted with the men whose names you mentioned, but I must confess I was at first afraid you were a spy."

" I thought that Young would not misinform me."

" No; Young is true as steel."

" He directed me to you as being able to accomplish more than any one here."

" These are the best imitations of the genuine bills I ever saw. None but the best judges could detect them."

" So *I* think myself. It costs a pile of money to engrave as good a plate as this, yet I believe I can realize a few thousand dollars out of it.

" I have no doubt you will do well with it. I don't know of anything of the kind now in St. Louis. I have a little bogus gold but have been dealing mostly in horses, and keep a livery stable. I buy horses very cheap of the boys; then fit them up to suit myself, and take them down the river to sell."

" Do you not occasionally have an owner come for a horse?"

" Not often! I have had as many as eighteen or twenty horses at one time, and never had one claimed. I usually keep them out of sight until I get them fitted for market, and changing their appearance as much as possible, I put them on board a steamboat, and run them down to the southern market. I remember once I got frightened; I took a horse of one of the boys, who had stolen him back in the country. Before I had time to fix up and dispose of the horse, the man who had stolen him was taken dangerously ill; his attending physician pronounced his disease incurable, and I was fearful that he would get frightened and confess every thing. In the meantime there was such close search for the horse, that I was compelled to keep him secreted; and I sheared and docked him, so as to change his appearance as much as possible. The fellow finally died, *good grit*, without blowing on anybody; and watching my opportunity, I got the horse down the river, sold him, and so the matter ended."

" Are you dealing in horses now, or don't the boys keep you well supplied?"

" Not very well at present. I got two horses a few days ago. One of the Longs, Fox, and Birch, came here with three good horses, a few days since, and left two of them with me. I had no suitable place to keep them, so I took them out a few miles, and put them in pasture."

" Young tells me that Fox and Birch are *game*."

" They are—no mistake."

" I would like to get acquainted with them. Don't you think they will want to get some of the paper? I should be glad to supply them, with any quantity, upon my return. I suppose they always have plenty of money?"

" They appear to be *flush*. I never saw Birch until he came here the other day with Fox and Long. Fox I have been acquainted with for a long time, and believe I know as much about his business as any other man. He has plenty of money—has always been very successful, and never spends much."

"What does he do with his money? I suppose, of course, he don't carry it about with him."

"He tells me that he has about two thousand dollars se-creted in the bluffs on the Des Moines River, in Iowa, con-cealed in four separate bottles, corked and sealed air-tight. Fox is the most energetic fellow I ever saw. He doesn't mind lying out three or four nights in succession to accom-plish his designs. Storms, cold, or heat, hunger, or fatigue, are all the same to him. When he once gets a good sight he never fails to raise it."

" Is John Long as much of a hero as Fox?"

" I am not as well acquainted with Long as with Fox. His physical powers are not equal to those of Fox, and he cannot endure as much."

" Where did they *raise* their horses, which they have left with you?"

" In the upper part of Missouri. The one they did not leave with me, was the finest race mare I ever saw in my life. Fox said he would not take a thousand dollars for her."

" Are the boys in St. Louis now?"

" No, not now."

" Where are they?"

" I don't know exactly."

"I wish I could find him. Fox seems to be a splendid fellow."

"Yes, and the others are of the *right stripe*."

"I suppose I cannot see them, then?"

"They left St. Louis in a hurry about the first day of August. I was up town and happening to come across the Chicago Democrat, read an article containing the disclosures of West, and implicating Fox, Long, and Birch, in several robberies on Rock River, and also expressing the opinion that they were concerned in the Davenport murder, on Rock Island. I carried the paper home and showed it to the boys. They left St. Louis, and crossed to Illinoistown the same day. Just at night, Fox returned after his race mare; he swore that his name should never be Fox, alias Sutton again and said they were all going east."

"Do you think they were concerned in the robbery and murder of Col. Davenport?"

"They did not tell me whether they did or not! I don't know anything about it."

"I suppose they are off on some good speculation?"

"Yes, Fox is always busy somewhere."

"How much of my paper shall I reserve for you when I return from Cincinnati?"

"If it is all as good as the sample, I shall want a considerable amount of it, but can't tell exactly how much. I am trying to get a tavern stand up street. If I succeed in that I shall want a big pile of it. Don't you want some of this gold?"

Reynolds handed me a counterfeit five dollar gold coin which I inspected.

"I think not at present. I would not dare to pass it while having all these blank bills in my possession. If I

should be arrested for passing the gold, and the bills found
on me, it would not be an easy matter to get out of the
scrape."

"You are right.   I like to see the boys cautious, yet I
would like to let you have a quantity of it, and we can
make it all right when you return from Cincinnati."

"I believe I will not meddle with it now."

After a pleasant half day's ride around the beautiful
environs of St. Louis, we returned to the city, the interview
having given me fresh track of the murderers.

After joining in a social glass of wine, and pledging myself to visit Mr. Reynolds on my return with the sixty
thousand dollars of counterfeit bank notes, I left him. I
communicated the intelligence received from Reynolds to
Dr. Reuben Knox, and also wrote to his brother at Rock
Island, informing him of the necessity of my proceeding to
Springfield, Illinois, to procure official documents.

Feeling a renewed confidence that I should succeed in
capturing the three murderers, I provided myself with three
pair of handcuffs for the purpose of harnessing the ruffians
whenever I might come up with them, and on the morning
of the 26th, I left St. Louis for Springfield, Illinois.

At Edwardsville, twenty miles from St. Louis, I met
with his excellency Governor Ford, of Illinois, on his way
from Springfield to St. Louis, to whom I presented a letter
of introduction from gentlemen of Rock Island.

Governor Ford informed me that he had received documents from that place by mail, in compliance with which,
requisitions were prepared and left with Hon. Thomas
Campbell, Secretary of State, subject to my order.

I had a long conversation with Governor Ford relative

to the murder of Col. Davenport, and the various schemes to attack and apprehend his murderers.

His excellency remarked that I was placing my own life in jeopardy in this adventure.

" I am aware of all the dangers attending such an undertaking, but so long as this formidable banditti are permitted to prey upon the community, no one is safe. I know that my life is in danger, but it is for the public as well as myself, that I incur the hazard. That man is unworthy the name and privileges of an American citizen, who shrinks back from any duty which he is called upon to perform by the voice of the community. Something must be done to check the ravages of this gang, and I for one had rather lose my life, in striving to protect the innocent and defenceless; than be slaughtered in cold blood like some of my neighbors."

" I assure you, sir, that I sincerely hope your efforts will prove successful."

Reaching Springfield, I found that requisitions were not prepared to the governors of all the States, I wished, and as there was great uncertainty as to where the murderers might be found, I obtained blank requisitions with Governor Ford's signature, under the seal of the State of Illinois, with power to fill the blanks with the name of any State in which I might wish to use them.

I was uncertain what course to take; but finally started for Terre Haute, and Indianapolis, Indiana. I reached Terre Haute on the 1st of September; feeling satisfied that I had missed the track, but not discouraged, as my former success in extracting information from members of the gang led me to feel certain of soon regaining the proper line of pursuit.

7

CHAPTER X.

CONTINUED PURSUIT OF THE MURDERERS.

AFTER much reflection, I at length determined to act upon the information received from Granville Young. Thus far, I had found his statements correct, and as he had referred me to old *John Birch*, the father of one of the murderers of whom I was in pursuit, and who resided at, or in the vicinity of Marshall, the county seat of Clark County, Illinois, I at once took passage for that place. Reaching it, I immediately disclosed the object of my journey to Wm. P. Bennett, Esq., Sheriff of the County, from whom I learned that the information I had received from Granville Young, relative to the residence and general reputation of John Birch, was correct.

"In this neighborhood," said the Sheriff, "Birch is almost universally known by the name of the 'Old Coon.'"

"Doubtless he deserves the appellation."

"He does, most certainly! Many traps have been set to ensnare him, but he has succeeded until this time in outwitting us all."

"Do you know his son?"

"Robert Birch? Yes, he is well known here; but dare not show himself in the county of Clark."

" I am inclined to think that he is concealed somewhere about his father's house."

" It would be well," said the Sheriff, " to watch the Old Coon's house secretly. If Robert is hidden there the appearance of a stranger might excite suspicion, and defeat his being discovered and arrested. The Old Coon,—the father, is one of the shrewdest, most cautious and cunning men in all the Northwest. He is said to have been well educated, yet he feigns unusual ignorance, and will never sign his name in any business transaction."

Sheriff Bennett's views were probably very judicious; notwithstanding, I determined to call upon the Old Coon, in his own house, believing that I could succeed in passing myself off as one of the gang with him, as well as with others.

The road from Marshall to the habitation of Old Birch, a distance of nine miles, led through an exceedingly dense forest, and by a blind path, to follow which was nearly impracticable to a stranger.

Sheriff Bennett kindly consented to accompany me a sufficient distance on my way to enable me to find the house. We traveled on horseback, and the Sheriff left me when we had come within half a mile of the house, and proceeded to a dense thicket in which he promised me that he would conceal himself and await my return.

Following the direction the Sheriff had given me, for a short distance, I emerged from the thick forest and entered a large and partially cultivated enclosure, near the centre of which stood a miserable log cabin in a very dilapidated condition, almost crumbling to the ground.

Leaving my horse at the edge of the wood, I approached the house cautiously on foot. The door was standing open, and within it, near the foot of the bed, sat a very old man. His appearance was wretched and poverty-stricken. An old woman and a young girl of sixteen were in the act of adjusting some portions of his dress, as I entered the room. Some bustle ensued upon my abrupt entrance. They however placed a stool for me to sit upon, and brought me some water to drink. I drank from a gourd shell, having a hole cut in its side; a very common substitute in some parts of our country for a dipper.

After some incidental conversation, the Old Coon, for it was Birch himself, upon whom I had intruded, inquired:

" Do you live in this part of the country? "

" No, I do not."

" Where do you, then?"

" In no particular place. I spend my time in traveling, speculating, etc.

"Do you want to see me? "

" Why, some of your old acquaintances wished me to call upon you, if I ever passed near you, and my business leading me this way, I have sought you out."

" Who do you mean?"

" Granville Young, and Bundy."

" How large a man is this Granville Young?"

" A small man, with dark hair."

" Are you acquainted with Owen Long?"

" Only by description," I replied, " I never saw him; but I know the boys."

" Do you? what! Aaron and John?"

" Yes."

" Aaron and John are Owen Long's sons. Owen Long and I were raised together in old North Carolina. I have known him ever since he was a boy. He's a right smart old man, and has got two smart boys."

" I think so. At least they know enough to take care of themselves."

" Well they do."

" I left my horse at the edge of the woods; let me step out and look to him."

Saying this, I winked to the old man who readily followed me out, and when we were out of hearing he said:

" Well, what is it, stranger?"

" The boys tell me that you are of the *right stripe*, and friendly to us, so I suppose I can safely proceed to disclose my business."

" I never hurts nobody."

" I felt certain that you were one of us! I have left the main travelled road because I promised the boys I would see you on my way down, and give you a little accommodation in my line. Look at these blank notes. They are a small sample of my work. I have a large amount to fill up and sign. I am now on my way to Cincinnati after it, and on my return shall wish to dispose of it. I suppose you can help me some."

" Yes, I'll take *right smart* of it myself. A heap of the boys stop with me, and I know of 'em, what will buy it, if you can sell it fair, I can get rid of a power of it."

" Do you think you could get a lot of horses with such paper as this, and have them delivered at Louisville or St. Louis?"

" Yes, and a smart chance of money too."

" Have you any confidential friends in this country who understand this business, and are acquainted with the boys?"

"Why, yes, I reckon so. There is one Mr. Arbuckle, at Marshall, and the *Clerk of our Court.* They both understand such matters, and are first rate men. I reckon they would like to trade with you."

"Are you suspected of being connected with the boys?"

"Not a bit of it. Any how I reckon not. The clerk is a good friend of mine and always tells me what is going on. They can't hurt the Old Coon, as long as he is Clerk of the Court. If the Sheriff should get a writ against me, the Clerk would let me know soon enough to let me get out of the way."

"Are you acquainted on East of us, so that you can tell me where to stop along my way. I have never travelled this way before, and don't know the boys."

"I know most on 'em," said the Old Coon, with a merry laugh, as if some pleasant memory came over his mind. "There is *Shack Phips, Hiram Long* and *Aaron,* cousins of John and Aaron Long—Old Owen Long and their father are brothers. They live in Owen County, Indiana, about fifty miles east of here. They are all good boys, but John Long is the smartest of the whole lot. He sticks to his friends and is right good grit. I will tell you what John did only last year. *Bundy* was in jail at Louisville, and would have gone to State Prison if no one had helped him. The boys were all afraid but John, to go to his assistance. He swore that he would not see a friend of his suffer while he could help him. After some exertion, he persuaded Granville Young to go with him to Louisville. Upon Bundy's trial they two swore him off clear, and he was acquitted. If John had been timid, like the other boys, Bundy would now be in jug."

"I would like two or three boys like John for partners in business. I don't know where John is now; I have not seen him in several months; probably he is up in Missouri."

"I have not seen him since last year."

"Nor heard from him, I suppose."

"No. Are you much acquainted in Missouri?"

"Yes, quite well along the river."

"Do you know a man by the name of Robert Birch? Robert H. Birch? he is my son; Robert is a smart fellow; do you know him?"

"I have heard the boys mention his name but have never seen him."

"He is a smart fellow, my son Robert is, you would like to know him, and travel with him."

"Well, I would."

"*He has traveled eight years.* Has got heaps of money. He never gets caught. He has not been at home in eight years. He wrote to me from St. Louis a few months ago, that he would be here before this time, but he has not come, I reckon he is making money. He and my son John left our homes in old Carolina together. John, poor fellow! they *hung* him in Texas. They just strung him up by the neck, without judge or jury, hung him like a dog; but they don't catch Robert.'·

By this time we had returned to the house, where we found the old man's son Tim Birch, who had just returned from the forest with his rifle. He was the youngest son of the Old Coon, and as his father proudly remarked to me, looked very much like Robert. Old Birch described the appearance of his favorite son at length, dwelling minutely upon his qualities and peculiarities. He was evidently very proud of that son of his, Robert. He very earnestly desired me to seize the first opportunity I might have to cultivate Robert's acquaintance, and associate myself with him.

I need not say that I very readily promised to become as intimate with him as possible.

The old woman and her daughter being informed that I was one of the boys, became very talkative. They were at least equal in wickedness, to any of the members of the gang of the other sex, and appeared much worse, for, as woman in her purity seems surpassingly lovely, so in her degradation she seems more than debased.

The old woman indulged in the most bitter denunciations against a certain neighbor of the Birch's, by the name of Miller. She swore some terrible vengeance against him. She would shoot him, chop him into mince-meat, etc., and all because Miller, as she said, had tried to have her Tim prosecuted just for stealing a miserable little colt, not worth thirty dollars; and she seemed also to believe that Miller was in some way instrumental in having John hung in Texas.

I was earnestly solicited by the family to remain a few days to recruit myself and horse. I was, however, satisfied that Robert Birch was not concealed in the vicinity of his father's residence, and that there was no prospect of my discovering any track of the murderers from the Old Coon.

Giving my name to them as Tom Brown, and promising to call on my return from Cincinnati, and spend more time with them, I left, having evidently satisfied the family that I was one of the boys, and a worthy associate of their son Robert.

I searched the thicket for my friend Sheriff Bennett, but he evidently supposing that I would remain with the Birchs all night, had returned home, leaving me to make the best of my way to Marshall, unassisted and alone.

Confiding, however, in my trusty horse, I was carried safely through the dense forest, and reached Marshall about midnight.

The following morning I disclosed as far as prudence dictated, the facts drawn out in my conversation with Old Birch. I also mentioned the character which the Old Coon gave of his neighbor Arbuckle, and of the Clerk of the Court.

Sheriff Bennett remarked that several criminal prosecutions had been brought in the County within the last three years, but from some cause heretofore unknown, the authorities had not been able to procure a conviction, but had never suspected anything wrong with the officers of the court.

The Sheriff promised to watch closely the movements of Old Birch and family, and to advise me of any appearance of the suspected individuals, and also keep an eye on Arbuckle and the Clerk of the Court.

I then left Marshall, and returned to Terre Haute, in which place I met with Mr. Hickox, Deputy Sheriff of Vigo County, Indiana. This gentleman informed me that a man calling his name Fox, had recently been arrested and committed to jail at Bowling Green, in Clay County, Indiana, on charge of horse stealing. From his description of the man, I had no doubt that he was the same Fox, suspected of participation in the murder of Col. Davenport. I at once procured a conveyance, and accompanied by Mr. Hickox, left Terre Haute for Bowling Green. The distance was only twenty-five miles, but as the roads proved to be extremely bad, we did not reach Bowling Green until the next morning.

On our arrival we learned that Fox had been arrested on suspicion of horse stealing, Shack Phips was also under arrest on a similar charge. Four horses had been taken from them, and detained as stolen. The owner of one of the horses had appeared and proved his property. Fox was examined before a magistrate, and held to bail in the sum of $800, in default of which he was committed to jail. Shack Phips was also held to bail in the sum of $400. His father entering bail for the amount, Shack was released. Fox remained in custody two weeks, when his father came and entered bail in the sum required, upon which he was also released. The three horses were retained in the custody of the officer, although there was no evidence of their being stolen.

When Fox was released on bail, he held a brief private conversation with his father in the street, and then left the village. His father settled his bill at the tavern, and returned to his residence, sixty-five miles east of Indianapolis, in Wayne County, Indiana.

As Fox had left town before his father, and in a different direction, all present track of him was fully obliterated.

I could discover nothing at Bowling Green of the whereabouts of John Long, or Birch, except the old Owen Long, formerly lived in Owen County, adjoining Clay. Some four years before, Owen Long with his two sons, John and Aaron was arrested on charge of breaking open and robbing a store. After a strict search, the goods were found under the floor of the old man's house. The three Longs were committed for trial, but broke jail and left the country, since which occurrence, nothing had been heard of any of them.

One of these horses taken from Fox, and detained, I readily recognized from description, as the race mare stolen in Missouri and described to me by Reynolds at St. Louis.

All track of the murderers had now disappeared. There was none of Long and Birch since they left St. Louis, and none of Fox since he left his father in the streets of Bowling Green, eight days ago. I felt quite confident, however, that Birch and Long were in the neighborhood at the time Fox was arrested, but had fled precipitately

Being unable to determine from my own reflection what course to pursue, I determined to take counsel with some of the prominent citizens of the place—with Messrs. Merryman, Elkin, Rose, Madesitt, (Clerk of the Circuit Court,) and the two Messrs. Osbone, to whom I disclosed the object of my mission. They all readily pledged themselves to render me any and every assistance in their power.

I learned from these gentlemen that Shack Phips, who was arrested with Fox, lived in Owen County, but a few miles distant in a sparsely settled country. Nearly all the settlers were connected in different ways with the Banditti. Phips had married a daughter of Widow Long, sister-in-law of Old Owen Long, and mother of Aaron and Hiram; all whose names I had taken from Granville Young or Old Birch. Phips lived in the house with Old Widow Long and her boys, and Fox had been arrested there.

Upon receiving this intelligence, I resolved to visit the settlement, and by stratagem get track of the murderers. When I proposed this, I was told that such efforts had already been made without success. That such an attempt would be dangerous in the extreme, and if the plot should be discovered by the gang, my death would be certain.

However, as no other plan suggested itself to my mind, by which the desired information could be obtained, I determined to make the attempt regardless of consequences.

In the meantime, I suggested that it would be well that the stolen horses taken from Fox, should be placed in my charge temporarily, as I might find them of assistance in my plans.

Addressing a letter to Mr. Knox, informing him of my present position, my doubts, and hopes, etc., I provided myself with a horse, and portmanteau well filled with articles of clothing, to give the impression that I was upon a long journey, and getting the necessary directions, I left Bowling Green for the Den of Thieves in Owen County.

CHAPTER XI.

SHACK PHIPS.

MY way towards the residence of Phips, was exceedingly devious, but after making the different angles until I was satisfied from the distance and description given to me, that I was in the neighborhood of Old Mother Long, as she was called, I ventured to inquire for Shack Phips, and was told that I was within one mile of his habitation.

"He lives," said my informant, "somewhat off from the road; he is not at home; you won't see him."

"If his wife is at home, it will answer my purpose just as well," I replied, asking for the direction.

"She lives at Old Mother Long's. You go on until you get to a small bridge crossing a ravine. Then turn into the woods at your right. You will find a by-path which, if you can follow, will lead you in sight of the house."

"Thank you, stranger."

"Are you acquainted with the Phips?"

"A friend of theirs," I replied.

Following the direction of my informant through a forest, thick with tangled underbrush, and nearly impenetrable, I presently emerged from a dense thicket, and found myself but a few rods distant from a miserable log cabin,

about fourteen feet square, with an open porch, or stoop;
the whole covered with rough clapboards, laid on loose,
and confined with small logs placed at equal distances apart
on the roof.

I dismounted at the edge of the forest, hitched my horse,
and walked to the house, where I found "Old Mother
Long," a meagre specimen of humanity, poorly clad, and
besmeared with dirt, and the wife of Shack Phips, a female
of about twenty years of age, of rather delicate features,
but whose whole appearance was very little, if any, superior to that of the old mother of the house.

The furniture consisted of crippled chairs, half a dozen
three-legged stools, two miserable beds; the bedsteads of
which were made of rough poles, with the bark still on; an
old rickety cupboard—a table made of a slab of timber,
roughly hewn; a couple of iron kettles, half a dozen broken
plates, as many knives and forks without handles, and a few
tin cups.

Seating myself on a stool, I inquired for Mr. Phips, and
was told that he was not at home.

"Is he expected soon? I would like to see him."

After watching me very sharply for a moment, as if to
read the object of my mission, Mrs. Phips inquired:

"Does Phips owe you anything?"

"No," I replied.

"Do you live about here?"

"No; I live more than two hundred miles distant."

"Are you acquainted with Phips?"

"No, I have never seen *him*, but I am well acquainted
with some of his friends, and as I am passing through the
country so near him, I thought I would call and see him."

"Do you know Judge Fox?" asked the old woman.

" Yes, very well, he is an intimate friend of mine."

" Is he? why Fox was here only a few days ago."

" Was he? indeed, I regret that I did not meet him, I have been looking for him for a month."

" Do you want to see Shack right bad?" asked his wife.

" Yes, I do."

" Well, I reckon I can holler him up."

Thus speaking, the lady left the house, and climbing up the gate post, commenced a "*yo ho a!*" at the top of her voice.

Shortly an answering shout was heard, and Phips emerged from the woods and entered the house.

He seemed somewhat startled and displeased at the sight of me, but after a few words of assurance from the old woman and his wife, that I was one of the boys, his good nature in a measure returned, although his speech was rather in the way of complaint of the ill-treatment of the public towards him, and I judge that he was by no means as well satisfied that I was one of the *right stripe*, as his family were.

" I am," he said, " an honest, hard working man, and was never guilty of a dishonest act in my life. I am poor, it is true, but I have always tried to get an honorable living. The people about Bowling Green are trying to ruin me. A man came here only a few days ago and sold me a horse. Soon after an owner came for the horse, and said it was stolen. I knew nothing about it. I paid the full value of the horse, but, because he was found in my possession, they took me up to Bowling Green, and put me in jail. All the folks at Bowling Green, are dead set against me, and I reckon I shall lose all I paid for the horse, as I don't know the man I bought him of."

Dark clouds appearing in the west, accompanied by loud thunder, gave me notice of an approaching storm. I started to put my horse under a shed which stood a short distance from the house, requesting Phips, in a careless tone of voice, to attend me.

Being desirous to bring my business to an issue, as soon as possible, I embraced the apportunity to introduce a few remarks that would enlist his confidence.

When a few rods from the house, I accosted him in a most familiar manner, and at the same time with a somewhat determined air.

"Phips!" said I, "it is all confounded nonsense to talk this kind of stuff to me. It is well enough to tell it to the folks about here, but I understand such matters, and will tell you my business at once. I came here to see if these horses which were taken from Fox, can be got and carried away from Bowling Green. Fox and I are old friends. I am traveling across the country from St. Louis to Cincinnati, and when I arrived at Terre Haute I heard that Fox had got into a bad scrape at Bowling Green, and I came up to see about it. I find that Fox has given bail and left, but they retain the horses. Now, if we can get the horses away before the owners call for them, there will not be sufficient evidence to convict Fox. He can then, you see, come back, stand his trial, and save eight hundred dollars, the amount of his bonds. If the horses are suffered to remain where they are until the owners come for them, Fox must sacrifice the amount of his bail, as you are aware that he cannot come and stand his trial with such evidence against him. It would send him to the Penitentiary at once, but if you will stand by me, and lend me a helping hand, I think we can get them away."

"How can we do it?" asked Phips, with a mingled ex-pression of fear and satisfaction.

"Easy enough!" I replied. "You must get some one to go and swear the horses are my property; and I will claim and take them away. I am a stranger to everybody there, and no one will suspect but what I am the real owner, and when the true owners come all they can say is, that some *rascal has got their horses and run with them,* but as they can't swear to the horses, unless they first find them, of course they cannot convict Fox, and I have no fear of their catching me or the horses, if I can get fifteen miles the start of them."

"All this is true, and I can get people to swear that the horses are yours. Still I am fearful they will not give them up."

"Why not?"

"Oh, I don't know, I was only expressing my fears."

"They must give them up. That is the only process I know of to recover stolen property."

"Will they not require you to enter into bonds to appear as witness against Fox at the next court?"

"I think not. You know I can promise to come, and not go."

"Yes, that is easy enough."

"Well, who will you get to swear that the horses are mine?"

"There are plenty of people in this neighborhood who will swear to anything."

"But it must be a person unknown to the authorities."

"True, it would not do to take any of my friends around here, but I can get lots of them down in Spice Valley."

"Where's that?"

8

" Eighty miles from here."

" That will consume too much time. I don't know how to be detained so long. I am in a great hurry to get through to Cincinnati; my speculation there ought to have been attended to before this time. However, I would not hesitate if I can do anything for Fox, at the risk of a day or two's delay."

" You are a true friend of his, no mistake."

" If we succeed in getting the horses away, we must leave the race mare where Fox can get her again."

" I am told that Fox would not take a thousand dollars for her. She is said to be the fastest quarter nag in the United States. By the way, do you know where Fox is now, so that we can send him word where to find the mare, if we succeed in getting her? "

" I don't know where he is now."

" The other horses are nothing extra. I will let some of the boys take them up north and sell them."

" I know Fox would like to get hold of the mare again, but at any rate, he wants the horses to be out of the way, so that they cannot be in evidence against him."

" What way did he suggest? I suppose one somewhat similar to my own? "

" No, he wanted me to go and burn the tavern barn, in which the horses are kept, the horses and all together; which would be getting them out of the way pretty effectually."

" Did you attempt it? "

" No, the people at Bowling Green keep such close watch that I dare not try it. If I was not certain that I should be the first one suspected, I would get some of the boys to do it, but I am afraid they would lynch me. A good many of

them had as lief hang me up to a tree without trial as any
other way."

" I think my plan much the best, and that would put an
end to it, without their supposing you have anything to do
with it."

" I think so, too. I am d——d glad that you called on
us. Nearly all the boys around here are afraid to do anything, if one of us happen to get into a scrape. If we only
had a few such fellows as you are, who would stick to us,
and help us out of trouble when we got caught, they would
soon get sick of troubling us. I wish you had time to go
down to Bloomington and see Esq. —— (mentioning a name
which I have forgotten.) He is a good lawyer, and a very
able man. He always helps us when we get into trouble.
He will ride day and night, and work every way in his
power to get us clear, and then he never charges us high
prices, and is willing to take his pay in horses, or any kind
of property we happen to have."

" He is a valuable member of the community."

" Yes, one of the finest fellows in the world."

" I cannot afford to be detained a sufficient length of time
to see him. We can get along without a lawyer just as
well, if you can find some one who is not known at Bowling
Green, to go before the authorities, and swear that the
horses are mine. Besides every day's delay is dangerous.
The owners may come for their horses. What is done
must be done in a hurry."

" There is Tim Birch, living about fifty miles from here,
we can get him."

" I have seen Tim. He is too young. If he is questioned
closely he may cross himself."

"He is a shrewd little devil—a chip of the old block. But there is his father, old John Birch. They can't cross him. He will swear to anything you tell him. The Old Coon they call him."

"Yes, I would be willing to risk the old man, but fifty miles is a long way to go and return. Here, continued I, (showing him my sheets of bank notes.) You see why I am in so much of a hurry. This is all ready to date and sign, and I ought to be in Cincinnati with it now."

"It is a splendid article," said Shack, examining it. "How much can you get like it?"

"About sixty thousand dollars."

"You are doing a big business."

"Yes, I am always doing something, and I would not be idling my time away now, if it were not to get Fox out of trouble."

"You are doing the fair thing by him, no mistake about that!"

"How did Fox get caught? I thought he was smart enough to take better care of himself."

"Fox, John Long, and Bob Birch came here together, with four horses, and staid a few days; I bought one of their horses. Hiram Long was negotiating a purchase of the other two, and Fox intended to take the race mare with him. John did not like to be seen about here on account of some old criminal charges against him in this county; so he and Birch left in the afternoon, and Fox intended to leave the next morning.

"That same night, a posse came from Bowling Green, arrested Fox and me, and took all the horses. The boys stole them in the western part of Illinois, and thought they were out of all danger with them here. The man who owned the horse which I had bought, got on their track, and had followed them as far as Bowling Green. Fox and I had been in Bowling Green with the horses, and mine was recognized at once by the man's description. That very night they came down and took us. If they had waited another day, Fox would have been off."

"I suppose you are well acquainted with the boys?"

"Yes, with Fox and John, but never saw Birch until he came here with them."

"What do you think of Birch?"

"He is a smart fellow, but rather too much of a fop to suit me. He had a fine gold watch and chain, and liked to show it often, and play with the chain."

"Fox is a man of the best judgment and intellect of all the boys. If John and Birch had followed his instructions they would not have been tracked. He told them to keep off from the main traveled roads with the horses, until they crossed the Wabash River, but after traveling about fifty miles from where they stole the horses, they took the highways; consequently there was no difficulty in tracking them. John Long is a bold, daring fellow, but he lacks prudence."

I was shown to a resting place in one corner of the room, and one of the three men pointed out to lodge with me, while the other two, with Phips, occupied a bed on the floor, made up with a few old quilts, and the two women occupied the other bed.

There being no light in the room, except the flickering blaze from a few dying embers on the hearth, I had no difficulty in arranging everything to my mind. I placed my portmanteau under the side of my bed, covered it with my coat and vest; placed my pistols and bowie knife where I could lay my hand upon them, and put my cane in the

foreside of my bed. Then, without divesting myself of my
clothing, but my coat and vest, I retired to bed for the night.
The man with whom I was to lodge had placed himself in
the back side of the bed, and all was now quiet.

I did not dare to go to sleep, for if suspected, I should
certainly be attacked before morning.

The threatening clouds, which had hung around the west,
at length had developed into a fearful storm, spreading
themselves in black array over the whole horizon. The
vivid lightning streamed forth in one continued blaze, succeeded by incessant crashes of terrific thunder, and the rain
fell in torrents.

The grim features of the ruffians, visible by the vivid
lightning streaming through the crevices in the walls of
the shattered fabric, served to complete a picture of fearful
interest to me.

The thoughts and reflections which crowded my mind, as
I lay amid those ruffians, seem to have made a singular and
ineffaceable impression. Years have passed since then, but
still as vividly as if of yesterday, do I recall the scenes of
that long, dismal and sleepless night.

CHAPTER XII.

DAY dawned at length; a bright and glorious morning rising over the darkness and storm of the dreary night.

The three men got up and left the house, and I saw no more of them.

The family soon after arose, and prepared a breakfast which I need not describe as it was but a continuation of the last night's supper.

About eight o'clock in the morning, while we were all sitting in the open porch before the cabin, a shrill whistle arose from the neighboring forest, like the long and quaviring cry of a wild turkey.

"There Shack, ——— you, you can start," said his gentle and affectionate wife.

"What is that?" I inquired.

"Hiram Long whistling for his grub," said Phips, starting for the woods with a readiness which proved his sympathy for Hiram's appetite.

After about an hour's absence, Phips returned.

He said he had told Hiram of my plans for recovering Fox's horses, and that he would be glad to see me, but dared not come to the house, and wished me to meet him in the woods.

"Go up past the stable yonder," said he, "to the corner of the fence, turn to the left into the woods, and whistle, and Hiram will answer you."

Taking my portmanteau on my arm, I followed the direction of Phips to the place designated, where I gave a clear, shrill whistle, which was answered from a dense thicket a few rods distant from me. I entered the thicket and found Hiram Long seated upon a log.

He was a small, well formed, and remarkably good looking young man of twenty-two or three years of age. His complexion was fair as that of a woman; his forehead prominent and high, while his full, clear, dark hazel eyes, and dark auburn hair made up one of the finest countenances I have ever seen.

From the manner of living, constantly in fear of pursuit and arrest for criminal offences, he had caught a sort of suspicious watchfulness, and was startled by every noise; his quick eye darting in every direction, seemed to catch every motion, and his practiced ear took in the slightest crackling of brush, or rustling of leaves.

After asking several questions which I answered to his satisfaction, we entered upon the important subject of getting the horses from Bowling Green. My plans as decribed to him by Phips appeared to meet his approbation.

"The Judge says he does not care for any of them but the race mare. If she can be secured so that he can get her, he will pay well for your trouble and delay."

"I know he will. If I can succeed in getting the horses as proposed, I will leave the mare about twenty miles above Terre Haute, near the Wabash River, where she can be secreted. Then I can send word to Fox where he can find ier, and hasten on to Cincinnati, where I must be as soon as possible."

" But," said Hiram, " if you are going to Cincinnati, it will not be much out of your way to go and see Fox."

" I do not know where he is now."

"He has gone to his father's in the eastern part of this State, and I think will remain at home until you can get there and see him."

It was with difficulty that I repressed a strong exclamation of pleasure at being told of the present lurking place of Fox, but endeavoring to conceal my satisfaction, I proceeded to remark upon the subject of the horses.

"It will require so much time to carry out our plans about the horses, that probably I shall not see Fox. If 1 succeed in getting them, you had better write to Fox, that he will find the mare, where 1 will leave her with a friend near the Wabash River."

" I will do so."

" And now about the witness to swear that the horses belong to me."

" You had better remain here, and send Phips after John Birch, the Old Coon: he will be the best witness I know of."

" That will consume a good deal of time. Let me suggest a plan. I believe they are getting a little sick of keeping the horses. Perhaps if I go and claim them as my property, I can get them without further trouble."

" I reckon not."

" I can try any way, and if they refuse to let the horses go, then we will send for Old Birch.

Hiram readily assented to the proposition, and I therefore, in order that I might fully impress the sincerity of my

designs upon the minds of Hiram Long and Phips, and
prevent all suspicion of me, requested that they would send
a spy to Bowling Green, that they might know if I suc·
ceeded in getting the horses, and if I did not I would then
return to them.

Having got track of Fox, the only object of my visit, I
was of course anxious to get away. Therefore, promising
Long to call upon him, on my return, and to furnish him
with a quantity of " *Rag Currency*," we separated.

I also made the same promise to Phips, who told me he
knew a great many who would like some of it.

" The Sheriff of Owen County," said he, " is one of our
friends, and a man of the *right stripe*. He always lets the
boys know if there is anything on foot against them. If
he had known when the posse came from Bowling Green
to arrest Fox and me, he would have given us timely
notice."

After bidding farewell to Shack's interesting family, and
receiving their best wishes for my success in securing the
horses, I started for Bowling Green, which place I reached
before nightfall.

At Bowling Green, I met with two men from Belville,
Illinois, in search of two of the horses. At my request,
they promised to keep their business secret for a short time,
I explaining to them my object in making the request, as
far as was necessary to gain their consent, and I then
got together the gentlemen with whom I had previously
consulted. I informed them of my success, telling them
that I had now only to take the horses away from Bowling
Green to accomplish my plans, and give me a clear track
of Fox. As the owner of the two horses had just arrived
with a witness to prove his property, I proposed that I

should assume the character of the owner of the horses, pay the charges for keeping them, take them out of the town, and then deliver them to the owner, who could proceed with them on his journey home. I would then take the race mare to Terre Haute, and leave her with Mr. Hickox, Deputy Sheriff, to await the order of the owner.

To all which the owner of the horses and all parties concerned readily assented.

One thing only remained to make the chain of action, thus far, perfect.

When Fox was arrested at Bowling Green, he employed a lawyer of that town by the name of Williamson, who was represented to me as a shrewd, cunning man, and a fine lawyer. Fearing that Williamson might have noticed our movements sufficiently to suspect that some trap was being laid for his client, Fox, and accordingly give him notice of the state of things in time to enable him to escape, I expressed a wish to see and converse with him before leaving the village.

The gentlemen with whom I was counselling opposed this, stating that Williamson was so remarkably keen, that they feared he would discover the plot.

I determined however to conduct the whole affair upon my own judgment, and despatched a messenger to Mr. Williamson, requesting him to call at the hotel as soon as his business would permit.

He soon after entered the bar-room where 1 was seated and in a hurried manner remarked:

" My name is Williamson; who is it that wishes to see me?"

" I am the person, sir," I replied, " have you a private room?"

" Yes, step up stairs."

When we were seated, I said: " I am informed, sir, that you are the attorney who defended my friend Fox, when he was arrested on charge of stealing these horses."

" I am, sir."

" Do you still consider yourself his lawyer? "

" Yes."

" Can I talk to you confidentially upon his business, and will you not betray me? "

" You can speak without fear or restraint upon any matter connected with Fox; but stop a moment."

Leaving his seat, the attorney subjected the neighboring rooms and closets to a close scrutiny; and then shutting the doors returned to his chair.

Seating myself at his side, I clapped my hand upon his knee, and looking him full in the face, continued:

" Mr. Williamson, I will disclose my business at once. I am a friend of Fox; while passing through the country near this point, I heard of his arrest, and the detention of these horses. I have come here for the purpose of getting them away. I have succeeded in the attempt to prove the horses to be my property; have got them into my possession, and am now about to leave town with them. Consequently you can inform Fox that he can come back, attend the court, and save his bail. I have got everything arranged, and shall be off in a few minutes with all the horses."

" By ——! That's a good one. I am glad you have succeeded in getting them. Be careful you are not suspected before you get away. I would not have the plot found out for five hundred dollars."

" There is no danger now. I have accomplished the most difficult part of the task. The people here think it is all right, and do not suspect my design. I have nothing to fear unless you betray me, and I am not much afraid of that."

" No, you need have no fears of me! It's the best trick I ever knew, by ——! I'ts d——d well done! I will tell you what I did before Fox left here. I wrote to Tom Rey nolds at St. Louis. Do you know him? "

" Yes, very well."

" Well, I wrote to Reynolds to send Myers, who you know is a noted horse jockey at St. Louis, down here to claim the horses, and get them away, if he should have to cut their throats the first night."

" Well, when Myers arrives, you can tell him that Jack Brown has saved him the trouble of getting the horses. I will leave the race mare in safe hands where Fox can get her, and then hasten on to Cincinnati, where I should be now."

" Fox is in Wayne County, Indiana, at his father's, not far from Centreville. You had better stop and see him, on your way."

" By the time I reach there, he may be off on some speculation."

" No; Fox will remain there until he hears from me what has been done with the horses."

" Well, I will call upon him, if it is not too far out of my way, but for fear I should not, you had better write, and let him know the particulars, and that he has nothing more to fear as far as the horses are concerned."

" I will write to him by next mail."

" After we leave the room, perhaps you had better not
speak to me, as you are known to have been the attorney
of Fox, and there might be some who would think it was
not all right."

" But they must know of our retiring together, and
holding a private conversation."

" True; we will say that my business with you was to
enquire if I was bound to pay the expense of keeping the
horses since they were taken from Fox."

" That will do, they shan't learn anything from me."

We then left the room and separated. I passed down
the hall stairs, and Williamson out of the back way, that
we might not be noticed together.

The news that the owner of the horses taken from Fox
had arrived, claimed, and proved his property, had now
become quite general, and a large number of citizens had
collected together to witness the departure of the horses.

Everybody appeared satisfied. The spy sent by Phips,
elated at my success in getting the horses without the
trouble of sending for Old Birch, hastened back to tell the
news. Williamson was gratified with the fortunate issue of
the trick to save his client from the punishment his crimes
so justly merited: and the public rejoiced that the rightful
owner had succeeded in recovering his stolen property,
while only the few to whom I had disclosed my real business
understood the farce.

Williamson approached me with a sly leer upon his astute
visage, and exclaimed:

" Those rogues have put you to a great deal of trouble
and expense."

" Very true, sir, but I am glad to get my horses any way."

I rode off, accompanied by the owner of the two horses,

in the presence of a large number of the citizens of Bowling Green.

After proceeding a short distance, I delivered the horses to their owner, and then hastened with the celebrated race nag to Terre Haute, where I arrived at eight o'clock the same evening, and placed the mare, as I had intended, under the charge of Mr. Hickox, Deputy Sheriff, to await the order of her owner from Missouri.

At one o'clock on the following morning I took the stage for Indianapolis.

Among the passengers in the stage coach was a very gentlemanly looking man, by the name of Adair, a son of the late Gov. Adair of Kentucky. While we were at breakfast, this gentleman remarked in the hearing of us all, that " a man had passed through Terre Haute in pursuit of the murderers of Col. George Davenport, of Rock Island; and from his success in tracking them thus far, the probability was he would eventually secure their arrest. The pursuit was conducted in a very secret manner, and but few knew of it."

" If such is the case, sir," I replied, " great caution should be used by all who are in the secret, as the murderers may hear the news, and make good their escape."

" Very true," he replied.

" But is there not some mistake about this? I have previously heard several similar reports."

" No," said Mr. Adair, " it is no mistake, I have it from Mr. Hickox, Deputy Sheriff at Terre Haute, who has seen and conversed with the man in pursuit."

" Does Mr. Hickox make the matter public to anybody and everybody? "

" No, he told me in confidence."

"Sir, are you not aware that you are abusing that confidence? If Mr. Hickox is in possession of such information *he* is censurable for making a confidant of any one, and *you*, sir, are equally censurable for betraying that confidence."

"What do you mean, sir? You are very free for a stranger! Do you intend an insult?"

"I mean just what I say. That Hickox is singularly imprudent, and that you are equally so."

"This is the first time I have mentioned it anywhere, and it can do no harm here."

"How do you know, sir, but some of the murderers or their friends may be present?"

"What! here? by no means! these are all gentlemen!"

"Are you acquainted with all present?"

"No. Nor do I wish to be. I know that they are all gentlemen."

"Are you not aware that either of these murderers might take passage in a stage coach, mingle with gentlemen, and appear in every respect as much like a gentleman as yourself?"

"What! a murderer! No, sir."

"Certainly he might; however, sir, allow me to inform you that *I* am the man spoken of by Mr. Hickox. It became necessary to disclose my business to him, as I was in need of his services, but he has no good apology for disclosing the secret."

"Is it possible? Are you the gentleman he spoke of? I had no idea there was any one present who had any knowledge of the matter."

"Either of the murderers might have been here as well as myself, and in making this matter public, you not only render the arrest of the murderers almost impossible, but you endanger my own life."

" I acknowledge the wrong, and beg pardon. I was imprudent, but did not consider the consequences which might result. I will be more cautious! Rest assured that I will not mention it hereafter."

The other passengers pledged themselves to keep the secret, and Mr. Adair, like a true gentleman, acknowledging that he had received a valuable lesson, the matter passed off smoothly.

On arriving at Indianapolis, a distance of seventy-five miles from Terre Haute, I met with Thomas B. Johnson, former U. S. Marshal of Iowa, under Harrison.

This meeting I considered a favorable circumstance, being confident of arresting Fox in Wayne County, at his father's; and having been at a loss in my reflections to determine what to do with him, while I should pursue John Long and Birch, of whom I had lost track since they left Old Mother Long's the day before Fox was arrested, and taken to Bowling Green.

Knowing Johnson as ex-Marshal of the District of Iowa, appeared to me a satisfactory reason for entrusting him with my secret, and endeavoring to secure his services.

He readily consented to accompany me to Wayne County, and if successful in arresting Fox, to take charge of him and follow my instructions for his safe keeping, while I should pursue Long and Birch.

At an early hour on the following morning we took stage for Centreville, the shire town of Wayne County, where we arrived the same evening, and ascertained that John Fox, father of William Fox, resided about nine miles southwest of the village. We were told that he was a

9

farmer of some wealth and of very industrious habits—of rough and uncouth manners, and poorly educated, but not suspected by any one of crime or dishonesty.

I disclosed my business to David Gentry, Esq., Sheriff of Wayne County, and to Thomas Noble, Clerk of the Court, both of whom rendered me valuable services.

Mr. Noble ascertained from a man living near old Mr. Fox, that William Fox was at home, and would remain there for several days, as he had not been at his father's home before for nine years.

I was now at a critical point of my adventure, as it seemed on the verge of success, yet with much remaining to be accomplished. I had no doubt of capturing Fox, but I had no track of Long and Birch. I was also anxious to get some clue to Fox's money on the Des Moines River in Iowa, feeling confident that the money of which Col. Davenport was robbed was concealed with it.

After much deliberation I resolved to draw this informa tion from Fox if possible, and also to obtain some track of Long and Birch.

This undertaking was one of peculiar difficulty—involv ing more danger and doubt than anything I had yet under- taken since the commencement of my perilous mission. Fox was not only a man of superior keenness and ability, but he had seen me when I was engaged in the Hodges' trial, and would no doubt recognize me at first sight.

Sheriff Gentry and Esquire Noble advised the immediate arrest of Fox, but this would prove fatal to any further track of Long and Birch, as also to the recovery of the money. I was compelled to differ in opinion from these gentlemen.

I therefore requested them to await my action for a short time before attempting the arrest.

Leaving Johnson at Centreville, I started alone on horseback for the residence of Mr. John Fox. Upon my arrival, I was told that William Fox was absent. After a short conversation with old Mr. Fox, during which I feigned much anxiety to continue on my journey, I departed, leaving a letter for William Fox, in which I signed my name as Thomas Brown, and stated that Reynolds had received a letter from Mr. Williamson, the attorney at Bowling Green in reference to the stolen horses. I alluded to the attorney's proposition to have Myers put in use, and proceeded to relate my success in obtaining the horses. I concluded by regretting that I could not see him as I must take stage at Centreville, for Cincinnati early on the succeeding morning.

My object in writing the above, as the reader will perceive, was to excite Fox's curiosity, and induce him to call upon me before I left Centreville; and to make the matter more certain I said to the old man, that if Fox would come for me in a wagon, I would return home with him, and stay until I had only time enough to intercept the stage for Cincinnati.

Returning at Centreville, I disclosed my plan to my associates, requesting them to be in readiness to act as circumstances might require, but to make no movement calculated to excite suspicion.

About ten o'clock at night, while standing in the shade of the lamp-post, in front of the tavern, Fox rode up to the door, leading a horse with a saddle on, and addressing the landlord, said:

" Is there a gentleman stopping with you by the name of Brown?"

" There was such a man here, but I think he has taken stage for Cincinnati. You can ascertain whether he has gone by stepping down to the stage office."

When Fox left, I requested the landlord to walk after him, and tell him that Mr. Brown was in his room, and to conduct him there.

Going up to my room, I threw myself carelessly upon my bed, and pretending to be nearly asleep, awaited the arrival of Fox. In a few minutes the landlord conducted him to my room and immediately withdrew.

As the murderer approached my bed, near which was a lighted candle, I leisurely raised myself and with a long yawn turned toward him.

Fox started back as he caught sight of my countenance, but recovering himself in a measure, said in a faltering voice—

" This is not Mr. Brown?"

" Not exactly."

" Is it not Mr. Bonney?"

" That's it, when I am at home," I replied, at the same time offering him my hand, which he took, although much excited.

I placed a chair for him near the stand, and placing myself opposite, said:

" Well, Fox, I suppose you did not expect to see me here?"

" No!" he replied, " I supposed it was Brown! but what brought you here?"

" We shall have but a short time to converse, as the stage will be here soon and I must leave for Cincinnati, so I will come to the matter at once. You will understand the object of my calling by the contents of my letter which 1 left with your father, over the signature of Tom Brown."

"Yes, I saw it."

"I presume you did not expect such a favor from me. At home I am Bonney; when traveling I am Brown, and as I know from good authority that you are one of the *right stripe*, I will speak freely. I have had a long chat with Reynolds in St. Louis, in consequence of which I recovered your horses, as you will learn from Williamson."

"It is true that I heard from him."

"He told me he should write you by the next mail."

"Bonney! you are the last man from whom I should have expected such a favor, or indeed one of any kind. But it was a d—d good move. The Bowling Green affair has vexed me exceedingly, but now I can go back and stand a trial."

"Exactly."

"When I first entered the room and recognized you, I thought a trap had been laid to catch me, but I am satisfied that all is right, or you would have known nothing of the letter from Williamson to Reynolds."

"Of course not. I knew that of itself would be sufficient to convince you, and now I will acquaint you with my business at Cincinnati."

As usual, I produced the sheets of bank notes.

"How do you like the article?"

Examining them closely, he said, "They are first rate."

"Better were never made."

"Where were they got up?"

"In Cincinnati."

"What amount have you?"

"Sixty thousand—only a sample with me, however. Would you like to get some when I return?"

"I might take some, although I don't like to traffic in such stuff. It is attended with a great deal of risk."

"Not with such an article as this."

"Perhaps not! By the way, Bonney! didn't you have something to do with the arrest and trial of the Hodges?"

"Certainly I did! They were charged with murder, which I oppose under all circumstances. There are ways enough for us boys to get money without killing men for it. I have no doubt you are as much opposed to murder as I am."

"Very true. I am!"

"If I had not thought so, I would not have exerted myself so much to free you from your Bowling Green difficulty. If I take a man's horse, he can buy another. If I take his money he can work and get more, but if I kill a man he is lost to his friends, and to the world."

"These are my sentiments."

"But anything else in the way of speculation, I am in for it. Now you understand me."

The reader will comprehend my object in assuming this position. Fox was well aware that I was active in the pursuit and arrest of the Hodges. I must therefore appear consistent with my former course of conduct, and at the same time manage to gain the confidence of Fox. I was very anxious to get some track of Long and Birch, and knew no other way except through Fox. He was not aware that he was suspected of any participation in the murder of Col. Davenport. At the close of our interview he seemed willing to give me his full confidence and urged me to accompany him to his father's, promising to furnish

me with a conveyance to Connersville in time for the stage
on the following morning.

Fearing that my inquiry at this time relative to Long and
Birch would arouse his suspicions, I determined to accompany him home.

As we passed from the room, I noticed that Johnson and
the Sheriff were ready with a posse to arrest my companion.
In consequence of a signal which I gave them, unnoticed
by Fox, we passed out of the house without interruption.

While Fox was getting his horses in readiness for our departure, I instructed Johnson to proceed early upon the following morning, with a posse to the residence of Old Mr.
Fox, and to arrest him and myself upon a feigned charge,
and commit us both to jail, where I would have an opportunity to extract such information as I might desire from
him relative to his comrades in the murder of Davenport,
and to the money concealed in the bluffs of the Des Moines
River.

We reached the old man's house about midnight, when
we retired to rest in the same bed.

In the morning I was kindly received by the family, and
treated with much courtesy. Had Fox been anything but
a cold-blooded murderer, I should have regretted the part I
was playing. I was in momentary expectation of the arrival of the Sheriff with the posse.

Breakfast being over, Fox prepared to accompany me to
Connersville. I was very much disconcerted that the posse
had not yet made its appearance, and was under the necessity of changing my previous arrangements. It being Sunday morning, I remarked that there might be some uncertainty about a stage from Connersville that day, when Fox

urged me to tarry until Monday morning, to which I assented with apparent reluctance.

During the day I was in constant expectation of the arrival of the posse, but from misunderstanding on the part of Johnson, they did not make their appearance. By this mistake, however, I was enabled to take advantage of managing a most interesting conversation with Fox.

Having gained his confidence in all matters except those in which murder was concerned, he conversed freely upon every minor subject connected with the operations of the gang.

My great object now being to gain intelligence of Long and Birch, my conversation had that constantly in view.

"I suppose, Fox," said I, "that you have been operating in this kind of business for a considerable length of time."

"Yes, about nine years."

"In what section of the country have you mostly traveled?"

"My line of operations has been from Wisconsin to Texas, in the states bordering on the Mississippi: generally near the river."

"You must have an extensive acquaintance with the boys?"

"Yes, I know hundreds of them! Some have fixed habitations: others travel, and operate where they can make the most money!"

"I would like to get some fellow who is well acquainted in the south and west to help me dispose of this paper, as soon as I can get it ready, and share in the profits. How would such a job suit you?"

"I don't like that kind of business. It is too dangerous. One is liable every moment to be detected."

" What kind of business do you prefer? "

" Robbing is much safer than counterfeiting. I can *raise* a thousand dollars with less risk of detection than there is in passing one counterfeit bill."

" If that is so much better and safer business, I would like to have a hand in it."

" I have friends in all parts of the country who keep a constant look-out, and when they find a good *sight*, they let me know; then I go and make the raise, pay them well for their trouble, and leave for some other part of the country as soon as possible. I have got thousands of dollars in this way, without being seen in the neighborhood where I made the raise."

" You must frequently incur a great deal of risk? "

" In most cases I can enter a house in the night, and search every part of it without giving any alarm."

" Is it possible? "

" Sometimes I get two or three of the boys in company with me, and enter a house in disguise, and boldly demand the money of the frightened household."

" But do they not sometimes refuse to give up their money, when demanded? "

" No. I never yet had any one refuse. They are always so d—dly frightened they are willing to give up their money, and glad to get off so."

" What would you do if they should refuse? "

" I would —— show a pistol or bowie-knife and threaten them, and if I could not frighten them to give up their money, I would let them go."

" I presume you have plenty of money, so that it would not have embarrassed you to have paid up your bail bonds at Bowling Green? "

"I could have paid much more than that amount without inconvenience. I have a good deal of money loaned out. Besides I have two thousand dollars buried."

"You have been very successful."

"Yes, and I have paid money enough to get some of my friends out of scrapes to make half a dozen men rich."

"Did you ever get caught before you were arrested at Bowling Green?"

"Yes; I was at Bellevue in Iowa, at the time the mob shot Brown. They arrested me at the same time, but could prove little or nothing against me. So they tied me up to a tree and whipped me nearly to death, and then let me go. Some of them may have to pay for it one of these days. I should not have been caught at Bowling Green if the boys had followed my advice."

"Were you acquainted with Brown who was killed at Bellevue?"

"Yes, my first horse was stolen under Brown's instructions."

"I presume that was not the last one."

"No. Not by fifty."

"Tom Reynolds told me that John Long and Bob Birch were with you when you left St. Louis. How happened it that they were not arrested with you?"

"They left Old Mother Long's where I was arrested, a few hours before the posse got there, and went down through Spice Valley to New Albany on the Ohio river, at which place they intended to take steamboat for Cincinnati."

"Then I may meet with them there. Do you think they would assist me in disposing of my counterfeit money?"

"If you happen to see them, I think they would; but

they will leave before you get there. They intended to stop in Cincinnati only a few days."

" Will they be near my route to or from Cincinnati, so that I can call and furnish them with a few thousand? It may be a benefit to them and me also. If so, I will call on them on my return."

" They will not be near your road. They have gone back into the country towards Cleveland."

" That would be entirely off my road. I am anxious to get back to St. Louis as soon as possible. Are you acquainted in Ohio? "

" I have never traveled in that State, but know some of our friends there? "

" Who do you know there? "

" *Helms*, who lives in Dresden on the Ohio Canal, is an extensive operator in our way, and *Norton B. Royce*, who lives in Illinois, on Rock River, is now in Ohio, twenty-four miles north of Columbus, and there are several others in Ohio, concerning whom, I am only acquainted through report."

" Are Long and Birch well acquainted up in Ohio, where they have gone? "

" They know Helms and Royce."

" They have gone to Dresden, I suppose."

" No; they are at Berkshire in Delaware County, at which place they agreed to meet Royce on the first of August, to make a small raise. They could not have got there by that time, but are probably there now, and have doubtless made the raise before this time."

" Who got up the sight for them? "

" Royce. He used to live there, and knew of some good sights, and told us if we would go out there, that we could raise three or four thousand dollars. Royce left Rock River early in July in order to get to Berkshire in time to make all necessary preliminary arrangements before our arrival. We were delayed on the way, and did not leave St. Louis until the first of August. Then I found a sight near the Wabash River, and concluded to return from Old Mother Long's and make that raise, while Birch and Long were to proceed to Ohio, join Royce, and raise what money they could there; then return and meet me on the Ohio River. Under this arrangement Long and Birch left Old Mother Long's before I was arrested. After I got out of jail at Bowling Green, I concluded to go home to father's on a visit and remain until I could hear what disposition was made of the horses. I am now expecting letters from Long and Birch telling me where to meet them."

CHAPTER XIII.

THE ARREST OF FOX.

AS the reader will have noticed, I allowed Fox to talk on in a loud and rambling manner, hoping that from all he said I should be able to extract such information as I desired.

"Who got up the sight for you on the Wabash River?" I inquired.

"*Jesse Ray!* an old acquaintance of ours, who keeps a station in Lawrence County, nine miles north of the county seat."

"Is it a good sight, and easy to raise?"

"It is small: only seven or eight hundred dollars. Ray gave me an accurate description of the premises, and location of the money. There is an old man living near Ray, who has at times loaned money to him, which in a few days he would return, noticing in what place the old man deposited it. Ray says the old man lives in a decayed log hut, some distance from neighbors, and keeps his money concealed in the under bed, on which the old man and his wife sleep. They are very pious people, and attend church regularly every Sunday. I intend to go on Saturday night, and secrete myself in a hazel thicket, a short distance from the house, and watch until the family are gone to church; then enter the house, rake down the money and put out with it."

" When you return to make that raise, you had better stop and get the race nag, as it will be but little out of your way."

" I don't like to take the race nag down that way again. They may be on the look out, and trouble me. I will send some one after her. I suppose it will be necessary for you to give me an order to get her, before you leave."

" You can't get her with an order."

" Why not?"

" I always look out for breakers. Some one, you know, might forge an order and get her. She is too valuable to lose, and I thought it well to guard against any trick."

" Can no one get her but yourself?"

" Any one directed by me can procure her."

" Tell me how if you please."

" First, you must know where to go, and then how to manage to get her, so if you send any person after her you must be very particular in giving directions."

" I am attentive."

" Go up the Wabash River, on the east side, twenty miles above Terre Haute. You will see a farm house and barn; the barn is set into a bank, with underground stables. Morrison is the name of the farmer. Enquire of him for a horse left there by a Mr. Brown. He will ask if you have an order from Mr. Brown, you will answer *No.* He will ask how do you expect me to give you the horse then? You will say, by giving the proper sign. He will say, what sign? Upon which you must cross your wrists at right angles, and repeat the words, *Robinson Crusoe*, when without further comment you will get your horse."

Fox was exceedingly amused at the novel sign, and watchword, and bursting into a fit of laughter, exclaimed, with a variety of oaths:

"Well, that's the ——— sign and watchword, I ever heard of. I never should have thought of that plan to pre. vent deception. *Bonney!* you are an *old one.*"

"After all the trouble I had taken to get the beast into my possession, I thought I would at least be smart enough to take care of her."

"Certainly."

"To what place will Long and Birch direct their letter when they write to you?"

"They will write to Ray, to tell me where to meet them when I go back to make that raise. I presume Ray has a letter from them before this time."

"Do Long and Birch understand their business sufficiently well to operate successfully?"

Yes, Long has travelled with me two years. He is a first-rate fellow, I never saw him stand back in a tight place. He would face the devil if it were necessary. I can always depend on him. If I send him to do a job, it is always done as well as if I were with him; but I have no confidence in Birch. He is too self-conceited. He wants to be called Captain, and has a deal to say in planning an expedition, but when he comes to a tight place, he always stands back, and says:

"*You* go ahead." It is not so with Long. The more difficult and hazardous the task, the more bold and desperate he is. I have had a great many partners during the last nine years, but John is the best partner I ever had. He is honorable, and can be depended upon. *I believe Birch would murder his best friend for two hundred dollars.* When we parted, I told John he had best get rid of Birch, but don't know whether he will.

"Have you ever been engaged in any robberies with Birch?"

"Yes, a large number. We were in a good many snaps up in Rock River, Illinois. Birch and I committed the robbery for which Bliss and Dewey were sent to the Penitentiary. Bliss had not the slightest knowledge of the transaction. Dewey, got up the sight, but took no further part in the robbery. I was also concerned in the robbery of Hascall, at Inlet Grove. I entered Hascall's house in the night during a terrible thunder storm, and took his trunk of money from under the bed in which himself and wife were lying together. They were awake at the time and conversing, while I was getting the trunk out from under the bed. The lightning shone so brightly that I could see every object in the room, yet I crawled upon the floor to the bed—secured the trunk and contents, and escaped undiscovered, and without causing the slightest alarm."

"Very skilfully done."

"Birch and I had the greatest time in attempting to rob Beach in Nauvoo. Amos Hodges ascertained that Beach had some four or five thousand dollars, and the whole plan was arranged—Hodges went to Brigham Young and got his opinion whether it would be right to rob Beach, as he was a brother Mormon. About this time Amos was compelled to leave Nauvoo, in consequence of some robberies in Iowa, in which he was implicated.

" It appeared that Brigham Young thought as Birch and I were not exactly Mormons, it would not answer to allow us to rob Beach, and accordingly told him of the whole plot. Beach got several men to help him guard his house, of which we were ignorant. On Sunday night, the time we had set for the robbery, Birch and I entered the house, and when in the act of taking a trunk containing the money, from the top of a bureau, we discovered the guard on the hall stairs, and at the same time were seen by them. We retreated, and rushed through the hall, where a part of the guard were stationed. Several guns were snapped at us, but fortunately the caps burst. They all pursued us, and as we were leaping the fence, two shots were fired at us. We ran as if the devil was after us, crossing streets, lots, through gardens, and over ditches, until they lost sight of us. In the flight I fell into a ditch of muddy water, and Birch lost one of his shoes, but we made good our escape; crossed the Mississippi River, and reached Old Redden's the same night."

" I suppose you have also been out with Long."

" Oh! yes. Long and I were concerned in the robbery of Frink & Walker's stage. In that we did not make much. We had expected to get hold of the Dixon land office money, but had been misinformed as to the time the receiver went to make his deposit."

" Are you acquainted with John Baker, who has traveled in the Rock River Country?"

" Yes; Baker and I traveled in company for two or three years, but we had a difficulty about some goods which we had raised from a peddler, at Troy Grove, in Illinois. I went south to spend the winter, and left the goods with

10

Baker to dispose of. When I returned he did not account for them to my satisfaction, so we dissolved partnership."

Thus the day wore away in conversation upon various topics connected with the gang, during which Fox said he had long been an intimate friend of Bridge, who has since been convicted as an accomplice in the Mulford robbery, and sentenced to the Penitentiary for a term of eight years. Fox stated that Bridge was owing him a large amount of money which he had loaned him at different times. Fox showed me a note for one hundred and sixty dollars, from which he said he had torn Bridge's name, after having heard of his arrest on charge of the Mulford robbery, fearing that suspicion might rest upon him as an accomplice, if the note should be found in his possession.

One little incident in my intercourse with Fox is worthy of mention, as showing how nearly my projects were defeated by a momentary carelessness on my own part.

While Fox was making his statements I had my memorandum book in my hand, taking down the names and place of residence of some of the gang, when the quick eye of Fox discovered in it a paper headed "REWARD."

" What is that reward? " he inquired with as little hesitation as possible.

I replied, "Only a reward offered for some runaway negroes."

At the same time, in an indifferent manner, I closed my memorandum book, and put it in my pocket, continuing the conversation upon the subject on which I had taken the memorandum.

This reward was, in fact, one offered for the " arrest of the murderers of Col. George Davenport," which I had imprudently placed in my memorandum book.

Having in this interview accomplished all that I desired relative to the track of Long and Birch, I retired to bed with Fox, as I had done on the previous night. I was still awaiting in anxious suspense for the arrival of the posse, but heard nothing from Johnson.

The care and anxiety under which I was laboring, did not prevent my sleeping soundly. I was worn out by fatigue, exposure and ill-health, and it was daylight before I awoke.

After breakfast Fox saddled his horses, and prepared to accompany me to Connersville, which he supposed I desired to reach in time for the morning stage to Cincinnati.

This did not exactly suit my plans, and accordingly as we were about to mount our horses, I again inquired the distance to Connersville, and also to Centreville, knowing them to be nearly equal. I therefore proposed to return to Centreville, and take stage from there for Cincinnati, instead of from Connersville.

Fox replied that he would accompany me to either place. We accordingly set out for Centreville, which we reached about nine o'clock in the morning.

At the hotel, I noticed Johnson with the Sheriff, and his posse, ready to make the arrest. I gave them the signal to hold back for the present.

Fox ordered his horses to the stable, and went down the street, to see an "old chum," saying that he would return within an hour.

This gave me all the time which I required to arrange my plans with Johnson and Sheriff Gentry.

I instructed Johnson to arrest Fox on a feigned charge of stealing a race horse in Missouri, and to arrest myself on a charge of counterfeiting. I requested him to have Fox very closely searched, in order to discover if he had any money, or other articles in his possession which were taken from Col. Davenport, at the time of the robbery and murder.

The blank sheets of bank notes, which would be found upon me would be sufficient to detain me to answer to the charge of counterfeiting. I would then give bail, while Johnson would place Fox in irons, and proceed with him to Indianapolis and confine him in jail. I would then proceed in my pursuit of Long and Birch, keep Fox entirely ignorant of the part I was acting, as also of the fact that he was at all suspected of the murder of Col. Davenport. I desired this course to be adopted for two reasons: First, that the gang should not learn that Fox was arrested on the charge of being concerned in the murder of Col. Davenport, as others connected with him in that affair would take fright and escape, before I could complete the campaign against Long and Birch, and secure the arrest of all the murderers.

My other reason was, that after capturing Long and Birch, it was my intention to return to Indianapolis, suffer myself to be thrown into the jail with Fox, on a feigned charge. I then intended to inform Fox that he was suspected of being one of the murderers of Col. Davenport, and that arrangements were in progress by means of which the authorities would convey him to Rock Island, to answer the charge before the proper legal tribunals.

At this stage of the plot, I intended, if Fox appeared sufficiently alarmed, to propose to him that he should bribe the jailor to let him escape, upon the payment of one thousand dollars. I knew that for the purpose of raising the proposed sum it would be necessary for Fox to have recourse to the sum of money which he had buried in the bluffs on the Des Moines river, in Iowa. In this way I hoped to draw from Fox a disclosure of the place of concealment of the money, and recover the amount of which Col. Davenport was robbed. I then intended to convey Fox, together with the other murderers, to Rock Island.

I had so far succeeded in my plot that I would have accomplished the whole scheme, if Johnson had been faithful, and followed my instructions as he had pledged himself to do.

Desiring to complete some further arrangements with Fox before his arrest, I requested Johnson and Gentry to delay it, until I should give them the signal.

When Fox returned to the hotel, I ordered a private room and some refreshments, over which we agreed upon an arrangement for future co-operation in business. I was to proceed to Cincinnati, finish and dispose of the sixty thousand dollars of counterfeit paper, and then return to the Wabash River, and get possession of the race nag.

Fox was to go and raise the sight got up by Ray, get discharged from his liabilities on the bail bonds, at Bowling Green, and then with John Long and Birch, meet me on the Canada line, from whence we were to proceed through Canada and the Eastern States, robbing, horse racing, etc.

All the time this arrangement was being fully determined upon, I was seated near the window of my room, from which I gave the signal for the arrest.

In a few moments a slight tap was heard at the door.

"I wish the chambermaid would leave my room alone until the stage leaves," I exclaimed. "She can then have it all to herself."

I opened the door as if to request her to leave, when Johnson at the head of a dozen men entered the room.

"There are the men! arrest them!" cried Johnson.

Several persons seized hold of me by the legs, arms and throat, while the others took possession of Fox in the same manner.

"What is the meaning of this, gentlemen?" I cried, endeavoring to break away from their hold.

"You will know soon enough."

They forced us hastily from the room; up a flight of stairs to the third story, and into the same room in which I had first met with Fox. There they stripped and searched us both.

Nothing was found upon the person of Fox except about fifty dollars in good money.

In searching me, they found a pair of rifle pistols—a revolving six-shooter, bowie-knife and dirk cane, together with the blank sheets and about three hundred dollars in notes, mostly on the State Bank of Missouri, some of which were judged to be bad, being precisely like the blank bills in my possession, on the same bank, which I had so often shown as samples of my sixty thousand dollars.

Thomas G. Noble, Esq., aided in the arrest and conducted the search. Several persons present, who were not in the secret of my plot, looked daggers at me, when the savage weapons and the blank bills were produced, forming, as they certainly did, very strong *prima facie* evidence of my guilt. I requested to see and consult with a lawyer, which, according to previous arrangement, was denied, both to Fox and myself. I did not wish my operations to be interfered with by any one, until I had brought Fox to the proper place to meet and defend the charges against him. I was too well aware of the quips and quirks of law, and had, I trust, an honest and well founded contempt of that class of lawyers whose trade it is, by means of their technical knowledge, to turn loose upon society men guilty of the blackest crimes, and, for a paltry fee, to aid in the escape from the just penalty of the law murderers and assassins. Such lawyers, if indeed they are worthy of the name, are the pests of society.

The poet has truly said, " An honest man is the noblest work of God." It may with equal truth be said, that an honest, high-minded and upright lawyer is the brightest ornament, as well as the most useful member of society; but where *one* such lawyer is found, a dozen of the other class will always be near to counteract his influence and destroy his power.

While we were undergoing the search, Johnson asked my name?

" Brown," I replied.

" Your name *may* be Brown, and it *may* be something else," said Johnson; " but, gentlemen, I have nothing to do with this Mr. Brown, as he calls himself. Appearances are against him, and I hope justice will be done him. I have a warrant for Mr. Fox, charging him with stealing a race horse in Missouri, and shall accordingly take him back with me."

All this had been previously arranged, and the words put in Johnson's mouth.

I replied to this: " That now the nag was taken from Fox—she was detained at Bowling Green for several days, but a short time since, a villian calling his name Jack Brown, came to Bowling Green, claimed the nag and took her away; but there is a man on his track, and I reckon he will have her by the time I get back."

Mr. Noble left the room, saying that he would go across

the street to the court house, where the Circuit Court was then in session, and ascertain what should be done with me.

By this time, the news that two blacklegs had been arrested, and were in custody at the hotel had become public in the street. Lawyers, from the court house, flocked to the door of the room for admission, hoping to secure a fee from the prisoners. Entrance being refused them, some appeared angry, while others walked away with the quiet indifference and composure characteristic of their profession.

Mr. Noble having returned, said:

" Mr. Brown, I have had your money examined. It is all good, except one ten dollar bill, which is pronounced counterfeit by the cashier of the Bank."

I started with astonishment, and asked him to show me the bill.

" Here," said he, " is your money, except the counterfeit bill, and the blank sheets, which I must detain until your case comes before the court. I am instructed to admit you to bail in the sum of one hundred dollars, conditional for your appearance at court from day to day, until your case is disposed of, in default of which you will be committed to await the action of the grand jury."

Some of those present exclaimed against the small sum required as bail.

" As but one counterfeit bill was found in the possession of Mr. Brown, and the court entertain some doubts whether the blank sheets could be considered as counterfeit, they never having been signed, therefore fixed the amount of bail at the sum of one hundred dollars."

I propose to deposit that sum of money with any good man, as collateral, who would be my security on the bond.

Mr. Noble replied, that he was clerk of the court; I might place that amount in his hands.

I expressed a disinclination to deposit the money with Noble, giving him to understand that I was afraid I should never get it again. Upon this he ordered me to be committed.

The bystanders assured me that the money would be safe in Mr. Noble's possession; that he was not only clerk of the court but an honorable man. I counted out the sum of one hundred dollars, and placed it in his hands, upon which I was released from custody, and left the room.

From the moment of our arrest up to the time that I gave bail, Fox was present, and every movement, thus far, had tended to pave the way for the full consummation of my plans with him. He had not uttered a word, but stood gazing upon the proceedings with an anxious eye, and a countenance as pale as death, through which, as through a transparent glass, shone the horrors of a guilty conscience.

After leaving the room in which Fox was confined, I made arrangements for his conveyance to Indianapolis without delay. A carriage was prepared, and Deputy Sheriff Pease engaged to accompany Johnson, with directions to crowd through at top speed, by changing horses at the stage stations, to prevent trouble or detention by habeas corpus, or other process, which would aid Fox to escape.

All things being properly arranged, Johnson and Pease left with Fox securely ironed, and under the most rigid instructions for his safe keeping.

I then despatched a letter to Joseph Knox, Esq., informing him of what had been done, and that I was about starting for Columbus, Ohio, on the track of Long and Birch.

I also requested the editors of the papers at Centreville, and at Richmond, to refrain from publishing the arrest of Fox.

I had thus secured the villain who I believed was the principal actor in the murder of Davenport. I considered that he was in safe hands, and that he could not by any possibility escape.

It was therefore with renewed hope and confidence of success that I proceeded on the track of Long and Birch.

CHAPTER XIV.

PURSUIT OF LONG AND BIRCH.

ON the night of September 8th, I left Centreville by stage, for Columbus, Ohio, at which place I arrived on the morning of the 10th. I visited the public hotels and examined the registers, but not finding the names of Long and Birch, or any track of them, I proceeded to the livery stable of General E. Gale, of Columbus, who dispatched a servant with horse and carriage, and conveyed me to Berkshire, in Delaware County, twenty-four miles north of' Columbus, which I reached late in the afternoon, after a ride of three hours, and stopped at a public house, kept by a Mr. Van Sickle, being the only tavern in the place.

After taking refreshment, I inquired after Norton B. Royce, of Illinois, and was told by Van Sickle that that individual had been staying with him for several weeks, but had just left for Illinois, having closed up his business in that part of the country.

I then inquired after two men, without mentioning their names, but describing Long and Birch, as minutely as possible.

After a pause, as if to summon something to his recollection, he replied:

" There were two men answering your description, who called here two weeks ago, traveling towards the East.

They said they were going by way of Pittsburgh across the mountains to New York."

This unfavorable intelligence somewhat confused me, and I was for the moment at a loss what course to pursue. During this moment of hesitation Van Sickle watched my countenance as if to divine my motive. He inquired whether or not I had any particular business with the men.

" I should have been very glad to have seen them. It would have been more for their advantage, however, than my own."

" It is very probable that you may ascertain the route they have taken, by going to the stage station."

I stood for a moment in deep thought, when recovering my self-possession, and presuming Van Sickle to be an honest man, I raised my eyes to his countenance, and was about to disclose my business to him, and explain the full guilt of the men of whom I was in pursuit, but a peculiar look in his eyes, a general expression of countenance, such as no honest man ever possessed, prevented the disclosure.

" My business," I said, " is not of a very urgent character. Some other time, perhaps, will do as well."

" If you were to tell me your business with them," said Van Sickle, " I may be able to inform them of it."

" Well, I suppose you may be trusted. These two men I wish to see, and myself, are joint owners of a fine race nag, now in Indiana. I have made up a race for a purse of five hundred dollars, which is to be run on the first day of next October. The smallest of these two men, whose name is Long, is well acquainted with the race nag, and has ridden her at several races, and I wanted him to ride this race now. Besides, as they are part owners of the nag, they would doubtless like to be present at the race.

However, as they have doubtless crossed the mountains, I may as well return and get some one else to ride her."

" I have no doubt," replied Van Sickle, " that these men are the same that you wish to see. I remember hearing them say something about owning a very valuable race mare, which they had left in Indiana. They must be the same ones."

" Well, when they return, tell them that I have called."

" They may be at Dresden, on the Ohio canal, now. Perhaps you can overtake them before they cross the mountains."

Suspecting by this time that Van Sickle was one of the boys, I ventured a bold question, and asked him:

" If Long and Birch had been speculating much in that part of the country."

" Not a great deal. They were not known by those names while stopping with me."

" Very likely not. We all of us find it convenient to change our names, to suit circumstances."

" Of course."

" By what names did they call themselves while here? "

" *Henderson* and *Blecher*."

" Yes; I have known them to travel under those names before. I suppose I must return without seeing them. Let me ask you one question before I go, however. " Van Sickle!" said I, addressing him familiarly, and tickling him on one side, " Don't you occasionally speculate a little yourself? "

" In what way do you mean? "

" Give me your solemn promise not to betray me, and I will speak more freely."

" Have no fears, I can keep a secret as well as any other man."

Taking my sheets of blank bills from my pockets, I showed them to him, asking:

" How do you like the looks of that article? "

" They look d——d well."

" Would you like some of it? "

" Have you plenty on hand? "

" Only a sample with me, but can get all that I want."

" I *would* like some; if they were only signed."

" When I reach Cincinnati, I can forward you as much as you please. You can use a large amount of it around this part of the country. You notice, it is nearly as good as the genuine bill."

" When you first called and inquired for Royce, and then for Long and Birch, I suspected you were an officer in pursuit of the boys for some offence, but no officer can track a man away from my house. Royce will be here this evening. He has not returned to Illinois as I told you, but has gone up into Marion County. He will return this evening."

" Are the other boys with him? "

" No. But they are not far off, Royce will know where they are."

" I think I can read a man's countenance. I knew you were one of our boys as soon as I saw you. I would like to see Royce, but can't stay now. Indeed I do not care particularly about it, unless Long can be got to ride the race nag. On the whole, I think I will return to Columbus this evening, and take to-morrow's stage for Indiana. As soon as the contemplated race is decided I must go to

Cincinnati, but will return this way and furnish you all you want in my line."

Of course it was not difficult for Van Sickle to persuade me to stay with him until the next day.

About dark Royce returned and was pointed out to me by Van Sickle. I introduced myself to him as an old acquaintance of Fox, and after some unimportant conversation, remarked:

" Mr. Royce, as Fox assured me that you were an old and intimate acquaintance of his, and of the right stripe, I shall take the liberty of speaking freely, and presume that I have nothing to fear in disclosing my business to you."

" I am very well acquainted with Fox. He told me that you and some of the boys were here operating a little, and requested me to call and ascertain how you are getting along."

" What is Fox doing now? "

"He was not doing anything when I left. He has had some trouble since Long and Birch separated from him. He was arrested with some horses that the boys raised near St. Louis, but is out now on bail. I have got the horses away, so that there is no evidence against him, and he will eventually get clear. He won't do much now until he hears from you and the boys. He told me that you had got up a few sights here, and that Long and Birch had come to help you raise them."

" Yes, but we have not accomplished much yet. Does Van Sickle know you? "

" I told him my name, and that I was after Long to ride their race nag, in a race to be run on the 1st of October next, for a purse of five hundred dollars, but I have told him nothing of yours or the boys business here.

" That was right. Van is a good fellow, but we dare not tell him all our affairs. He is not sufficiently discreet."

" As regards my own business at this time, I am getting up a large amount of rag currency at Cincinnati, of which I have a sample," producing my blank sheets. " Fox told me that as you had probably made a raise of three sights, and would therefore be flush with funds, you might want a large amount of goods in my line, for which reason I thought best to call upon you on my way to Cincinnati. I shall have about sixty thousand dollars ready, as soon as two men can date and sign the bills. I would like very well to show Long and Birch a sample, and ascertain how much of it they will take."

" The boys are forty or fifty miles from here now, and have accomplished nothing since coming into this part of the country. They promised to meet me here on the 1st of August, but did not, in consequence of which we have lost two good sights. I had an old aunt here, who lately sold her property for twenty-two hundred dollars in gold. If the boys had been here, we could have raised all that without the least difficulty, but she left about the 10th of August, went West, and paid out her money for a new home. Then there was a merchant one mile north of this place, who had eighteen hundred dollars in his trunk, with which he started to purchase goods in New York, leaving here about the middle of August.

" These two sights, making four thousand dollars, we might as well have had as not. As it is, we have lost the whole. The boys however, are out making arrangements to raise another sight we have on hand."

" Is this last a good sight? "

" Pretty fair. We expect to raise about sixteen hundred dollars."

" What direction is it from here? "

" Nearly a north course. In the northwest corner of Knox, on the edge of Marion county."

" How are things situated? Will they get the money without difficulty? "

" Yes, the owner is an old Jersey farmer. He has only a small family, and lives at a considerable distance from any neighbors, in a small frame house, the doors of which he never fastens. The boys went up to make the raise about ten days ago, but there was a camp meeting in the neighbor. hood, and some of the brethren were staying with this family every night. Consequently they thought best to re- turn, and wait until the camp meeting was over, and now they are on their second tour of observation. I have been up myself to see them once since they left, and discovered that they were getting along finely. They have examined the premises during the night, and Long raised the door latch, and opened the door, which was not fastened

" Where do they stay, while making arrangments to raise the money? "

" In the woods, and in hay stacks near by the house. There is a large corn-field extending from the house to the neighboring forest, providing ample cover to and from the dwelling. I saw them night before last, and left provisions with them sufficient for four or five days, when I shall see them again."

" Do they know the situation of the rooms in the house? "

" Yes, during the season of the camp meeting Long went to the house and asked to stay over night, but was refused because they were full of the preachers. Long, however,

11

discovered that there were but two rooms in the house. The family sleep in the apartment occupied for a kitchen."

"Did you learn the old man's name? "

"Yes; but I have forgotten it. It was something like Black, Blackman or Blackburn."

"Will you see them again before they make the raise?"

"Yes; Saturday night next, I have promised to carry them more provisions. We have agreed on a place to meet at precisely twelve o'clock at night. I shall then learn more about the matter, and if everything is right we shall make the raise on Sunday night."

" I presume you will leave this part of the country as soon as possible after making the raise, traveling during the night to avoid pursuit."

" Yes; we always travel as far from the vicinity of a transaction as possible the first night after making a raise. We then conceal ourselves during the succeeding day, proceed again under the cover of night until we get beyond the reach of suspicion. In this way there is no danger of detection."

" Will you have help enough to make the raise in case you should meet with opposition? "

"I think we shall. No better men than John and Birch ever yet followed up a sight and we shall all be well armed.'

" I would like to meet with you, and the boys, at some suitable place, as soon as convenient, after you have made this raise. If the boys have good luck in it, they will then be prepared to purchase a quantity of my rag money. It will take but a short time to sign and date it, and it will then be ready for use."

" We will meet you wherever you please. We have no other sights to raise in this vicinity, and it will make no difference with any of us, in which way we go after leaving here. So suit yourself as to place of meeting."

"If I knew exactly the length of time I shall be detained at Cincinnati, I could better determine when and where to meet you, but we must come to some definite understanding before I return. I am somewhat fearful too, that you have not help enough to make the raise."

"We thought so ourselves at first, and Long went out to Dresden to get Helms to help us, but he was not at home, and we concluded after examining the house, and noticing the situation of the family, that our force was sufficient."

Much more conversation passed between us upon this and various other operations of the gang until late at night, when we separated.

Notwithstanding the great fatigue of traveling by stage day and night, involving loss of sleep, the present crisis was one of too much importance, and too much remained still to be accomplished, to permit me to spare even the time necessary to renovate exhausted nature. Sleep departed from me, and a variety of expedients crowded at once upon my troubled mind. I had no difficulty in fixing upon a time and place to meet with and capture Royce, Long, and Birch, after the commission of their contemplated robbery, but as I lay in the deep silence of night, it seemed as if there passed before my mental eye the bloody scenes enacted at the late residence of Miller and Liecy, and in the halls of the lamented Davenport. I felt that in the quiet farm house of the worthy old Jerseyman, similar scenes were about to take place, and it was my duty to endeavor at least to prevent the villains from succeeding in their attempt.

After spending a long and sleepless night and discussing various projects, weighing each in all the bearings I could think of, I at length decided upon one likely to prove successful in preventing this new robbery, and saving the unsuspecting family of the farmer from their danger, and at the same time enable me to capture the wretches.

My plan was, to endeavor by proposing a more brilliant operation than the one they had in view, to detach them from the pursuit of the one, on the ground of its little comparative importance.

In the morning I held another interview with Royce, and commenced at once upon my plan.

"Royce, I have long had a plot in contemplation, which, if carried into execution, will make four or five men rich, and the difficulty of getting men to assist me, in whom I can place implicit confidence, has as yet deterred me from executing my project; and I now seldom mention the subject to any one. Fox, however, has assured me that you are a man who may be fully trusted, and I will give you the outlines of the plot, which is, to rob the vaults of a bank containing about eighty thousand dollars."

"If that can be done, it is just the speculation I would like to engage in."

"It can be done with perfect safety. This thing of making small raises about the country is poor business. They are attended with too much risk for the profit they yield. A man who hazards his life and liberty ought to do it for an adequate result. Besides there is no more danger of detection in raising eighty thousand dollars than one thousand. To carry out the plan I speak of successfully, will require four or five resolute, skillful and energetic men. Fox will go with me whenever I say the word, and I want no better man. He is the only one as yet whom I have selected to accompany me in the expedition. From his recommendation, although I am unacquainted with you, I would be willing that you should be one of the number. Then we ought to have one or two more to operate effectually. But at present, I am engaged in this matter at Cincinnati, and must attend to it in preference to any speculation."

" Why not get Long and Birch to make out the number? Then we could go into this bank speculation as soon as you can get your counterfeit paper disposed of."

" I am not sufficiently acquainted with Long and Birch, to trust them in an enterprise of so much importance. I must have men who will stand by me in any emergency, and follow my instructions to the letter."

" We can't find better men for such an operation than Long and Birch. I have known them for a long time, and have been with them in a good many tight places. I never knew them to flinch. If practice is worth anything, they ought to be perfect, for they have been in such business for several years, and have always been successful. As far as my opinion is worth anything, I would as soon trust them as Fox. They are men as good and true as he, and understand the business as well."

" Upon your recommendation, and what I have heard Fox say of them, I think I might safely include them in the number. They must, however, first pledge themselves to follow my counsel in every respect. I have been at much expense and trouble to learn the situation of the vault, and all things connected with the internal situation of the banking house. Do you think they would be willing to engage in the adventure on such terms? "

"Nothing would suit them better. Where is the bank, and how is it situated?"

"It is the South Bend Bank, in the State of Indiana. Were you ever there?"

"No; I have heard of it though. How can we enter the vault, and secure the money?"

"By undermining the walls, and going in through the floor. We can then seize the boxes containing the specie and bank notes, and make off with them."

"How soon will you be in readiness to make this bank raise?"

"If I wait to get through with my present speculation, it will be at least four weeks, but since we have been talking, I have thought of a different plan. You, Long and Birch, and myself are now here together. Fox is within two hundred miles of us. Perhaps I had better return to Cincinnati, get the men at work, filling up and signing these bills, and then return by way of Indiana, where I will pick up Fox; while you and the boys, in the mean time, can make this raise of the old Jersey farmer; then we will all meet at some place, upon which we can mutually agree, and go and rob the bank, while my men are filling up the blank bills. How will that suit you?"

"Exactly. We will meet you at any place you will designate."

"As this robbery of the old farmer will naturally create great excitement in this vicinity, we must meet at some remote point. However, as this raise of yours is of little consequence compared with my sight on the South Bend Bank, I would suggest the policy of abandoning it, until we have disposed of my operation. You can then come back and make this raise, while I proceed to Cincinnati after

my paper, which by that time will be completed. I can
then supply you and the boys with any amount you want,
and then we can each go our own way."

"Your idea is certainly a good one. I think the boys
will agree with us, and abandon the sight they are on for
yours. Where shall we meet?"

"When you see the boys, first find out if they are willing
to leave their present sight for mine. If they will not, our
place for meeting must be far from here. I think Adrian,
Michigan, will be a good point, as it is directly on our road
to South Bend."

"How long will it detain you to do your business in Cincinnati, go after Fox and get around to Adrian?"

"To-day is Wednesday. I can reach Cincinnati to-
morrow, remain there two days, which will occupy the
remainder of this week. I will then go from Cincinnati,
get Fox and meet you at Adrian next week on Saturday.
Will you be there with Long and Birch on that day? If
so, I will be punctual to the time."

"We will be there without fail. I will go and meet
Long and Birch, on Saturday night; tell them the whole
arrangment and advise them to abandon their sight for yours,
and we will have sufficient time to arrive at Adrian at the
time you propose."

"Then let that be the understanding, and I shall not expect to see you again until we meet at Adrian. I shall not
return this way, as it will be much nearer for Fox and myself to go from his father's, in Wayne County, direct to
Adrian. You and the boys must do as you think proper
about raking down the old Jersey farmer, before you start
for South Bend, but you have *my* opinion, that it would be

advisable to defer it. Tell the boys *Tom Brown* is on hand."

Then taking a social glass of wine with him and Van Sickle, and promising to call as often as in my power, and to furnish Van Sickle with a good supply of the " *ready*," and wishing each other success, with a hearty shaking of hands I took leave of Berkshire for Columbus, at which place I arrived about the middle of the day.

Believing the plot I had arranged sufficient to place Long and Birch in a situation where I could capture them, the only fears I entertained were, that they might yet decide to rob, and perhaps murder the old Jersey farmer, before leaving that vicinity. I therefore proposed to intercept and arrest them in time to save the family, in case they should make such an attempt, and if not, to seize them on their way to Adrian, before they should cross the State line into Michigan.

After filling the blanks in the requisitions of the Governor of Illinois I proceeded to the office of the Secretary of State, to obtain writs from the Governor of Ohio, for the arrest of Long and Birch. The Governor and Secretary of State being absent, I applied to Mr. Woods, State Auditor, who was authorized by the Governor to transact such business in his absence from the seat of government.

After much difficulty and no little persuasion, I obtained from Mr. Woods the writs necessary for the arrest; not however until I had convinced that honorable gentleman that, if the individuals for whom I held requisitions, were suffered to remain in the neighboring county a few days longer, the inhabitants would be glad to get rid of them on any terms, even if they applied the Lynch law.

After obtaining the requisite official documents I procured the services of E. Gale, Esq., of Columbus, late Adjutant General of the State of Ohio, who accompanied me that same night to Mount Vernon, the seat of justice for Knox County, a distance of forty-five miles.

The following morning we visited the collector's office to ascertain if a person by the name Royce had given us as that of the Jersey farmer, resided in the northwest part of Knox County, and also to learn his reputed circumstances. We determined to reach the abode of the farmer in time to protect his family from their impending fate.

We found upon the assessment roll of Knox County, all the names which had been mentioned by Royce, and we learned upon further inquiry, that a camp meeting had recently been held in the northwest corner of Knox County. This intelligence convinced me that the statements of Royce were correct, and I accordingly employed A. Thrift, Esq., Sheriff of the County, to accompany us, and disclosed to him and to General Gale, as much of my business as I deemed prudent or necessary at the time.

Before leaving Columbus for Mount Vernon, the State Auditor, Mr. Woods, furnished me with a letter of introduction to A. B. Curtiss, Esq., of the latter place, recommending me to his favorable notice and assistance.

We left Mount Vernon in pursuit of the murderers; passed through Frederick, Middlebury, Franklin, and Chesterville to Mount Gilead in Marion County, but not finding the name, place, or description to correspond with our previous information, we stopped for the night, hoping that some new intelligence might be obtained.

During the evening, I was introduced by Sheriff Thrift to a certain Mr. Shaw, a member of the Ohio Legislature

from the County of Marion, to whom I disclosed the outlines of my business.   This gentleman stated that he knew
of a Mr. Black, who resided a few miles distant from Mount
Gilead, and who, judging from the description of his family
and location of his premises, was probably the farmer whom
the robbers intended to molest.

At my request, Mr. Shaw accompanied us to the house
of Mr. Black on the following morning, to whom I pro-
pounded some indirect inquiries.   Suddenly our new associate, Mr. Shaw, became restless, evincing symptoms of
alarm, and hurriedly swallowing a glass of water, departed.
I was at a loss to account for the cause of his fear, but supposed he was seized with a momentary panic at the idea of
the immediate neighborhood of bloody and remorseless
robbers, and believing, like worthy John Falstaff, that
prudence is the better part of valor, chose to make a safe
retreat.

A few moments' conversation with Mr. Black, and an
investigation of his premises, convinced me that he was not
the selected victim.   Picking up Mr. Shaw, we persuaded
him to accompany us a few miles further, to the town of
Galleon, in Richland County, where, being satisfied that he
was not the soldier for this kind of warfare, we did not
urge him to go with us further, and he returned to Mount
Gilead.

From Galleon we proceeded by a circuitous route to
Johnsville without getting any trace of the villains.   After
two or three days spent in investigation and inquiry, we
became well satisfied that the robbery of the Jersey farmer
was deferred to prepare for the South Bend Bank robbery,
and I congratulated myself that my plot to rescue the un-

suspecting family from the grasp of the assassins had proved successful.

Having already obtained writs from the Governor the next move in order was, to intercept and arrest the murderers before reaching the Michigan State line, on their way to Adrian.

If I should fail in this attempt, and find it necessary to meet them at Adrian, another obstacle would remain to be overcome. In accordance with the arrangements I had made with Royce, I should be compelled to bring Fox with me. I knew that Long and Birch were old and experienced "*rats*," and I was fearful that they would suspect a trap and guard against being decoyed into it, by sending Royce in advance, to see if Fox should make his appearance in company with *Tom Brown*, which latter gentleman they were acquainted with only by reputation. In such a case it would be necessary to account satisfactorily for the absence of Fox.

To prepare for this emergency, I wrote the following handbill:

LOOK OUT FOR HORSE THIEVES !!

" On, or about the 10th day of September, a man by the name of William Fox was arrested near Bowling Green, having in his possession three stolen horses. He gave bail for his appearance at the next term of the court in the sum of eight hundred dollars, and left the country.

" A few days afterwards a man calling his name *Jack Brown*, made his appearance, proved a claim upon the horses, and took them away. In a few days the real owners of the horses appeared, but nothing could be heard either of them or of Jack Brown, who it is supposed has gone to Cincinnati.

" The public would do well to be on the lookout, as a

gang of horse thieves are in our midst."— *Wabash En-quirer.*

I took this article to a printing office, and had it struck off upon a piece of newspaper which was printed on the opposite side. Then by trimming the edges, I gave it the appearance of having been cut from a newspaper, and placed it carefully in my pocket to use as circumstances might require.

CHAPTER XV.

WE left Mount Vernon and returned through Frederick and Sparta to Berkshire, the residence of Van Sickle.

Before reaching Berkshire, Sheriff Thrift, who was known to Van Sickle, left us and took another route, by which he reached that place late in the evening, and feigned to be an entire stranger to General Gale and myself.

Soon after Thrift's appearance, Van Sickle took me one side and informed me that the gentleman who had just arrived was the Sheriff of Knox County, and wondered what his business was at that place.

I quieted his fears by suggesting that he was probably on his way to Columbus, and that at any rate, he could bave no business with me, as I was a stranger in that part of the country. I inquired if Royce had started on his return to Illinois, and was answered in the affirmative. He also stated that he had not heard of Long and Birch since I left.

I promised to visit Van Sickle again after getting my counterfeit paper finished, and after attending the horse race in Indiana.

While at this place, Thrift, Gale and myself treated each other as strangers, and we left together the following morning, as if accidentally.

We proceeded to Delaware; thence to Marion, the seat of Marion County; thence to Little Sandusky, at which place we met with *Birch*, on the race course, betting and gambling. He wore in plain view the gold watch-chain, and seal which were taken from Col. Davenport when he was murdered at Rock Island, and of which I had an accurate description in my pocket. Neither Royce nor Long was with him, and to have arrested him would have been to let Long escape. Besides, he was doubtless on his way to Adrian, and would join his confederates before reaching that place.

Without making our business known to anyone, or instituting any inquiry, we left Birch on the race course, and passed on a distance of seven miles, to Upper Sandusky. I had sufficient knowledge of the geography of the country to know Long and Birch would, on their way to Adrian, either pass through Lower Sandusky, or leave that place on the right, and cross the Maumee River at Perrysburgh. I therefore aimed to intercept them at one of these two points, and to take them to Rock Island by way of Detroit, St. Joseph and Chicago.

I at this time wrote to Johnson, at Indianapolis, to proceed with Fox to Springfield, Illinois.

I took stage at Upper Sandusky, accompanied by Sheriff Thrift, to Tiffin; thence by railroad to Belleview in Huron County, at which place I found time to address a letter to Joseph Knox, Esq., of Rock Island, giving him a minute account of the progress I had made since succeeding in the arrest of Fox.

We arrived at Lower Sandusky early on the morning of the 18th. I called on Mr. Dickinson, acquainted him with the particulars of my business, gave him the names under which Long and Birch were traveling—*Henderson* and *Blecher*—and made every arrangement with him for their arrest, if they should pass through Lower Sandusky on their way to Adrian. I supposed it probable that they would reach this place in the afternoon stage, from Little Sandusky. After completing this arrangement the Sheriff and myself took stage for Perrysburgh, a distance of thirty miles, for the purpose of guarding that point, and intercepting the murderers, if they should pass Lower Sandusky.

About fifteen miles distant from this latter place, I recognized Royce a little ways in advance of the stage, traveling on foot, with a portmanteau on his shoulder. I had barely time to say to Sheriff Thrift, " Treat me as a stranger," when the stage came up with him. I beckoned to him, and the stage stopped to receive him. No questions were asked until we reached Howards' Hotel, nine miles east of Perrysburgh, when the stage made a halt, and we dismounted. Royce inquired for Fox, and wished to know why he was not with me. He was also anxious to know who the gentleman with me was.

I replied that he was a stranger to me, and that I had narrowly escaped detection and arrest for getting the horses from Bowling Green, and was forced to flee for safety. I promised to give him the particulars as soon as an opportunity could be had after reaching Perrysburgh. I then inquired for Long and Birch. Royce said they were coming on, and would meet him at the American Hotel in Perrysburgh that evening. I told him, that as we ought to avoid being seen in company, I would stop at the other

house, while he and the boys might meet at the American
Hotel, when I would call upon them and prepare to go on
to Adrian in company.

At Perrysburgh, I stopped with Sheriff Thrift at the
Stage House, for the purpose of making arrangements unknown to Royce for the arrest of Long and Birch immediately after their arrival.

I called to my assistance J. C. Spink, Esq., to whom I
had been referred by Mr. Dickinson, and our preparations
were speedily made for the reception of the murderers.

I then held an interview with Royce, who at first manifested much distrust because Fox was not with me. I was
obliged to manufacture a story to quiet his suspicions. I
told him that after leaving him at Berkshire, I had returned
to Columbus, and from thence to Cincinnati. I had there
stepped into a reading room and seen an article copied from
the Wabash Enquirer, headed, " Look out for horse
thieves," and speaking of me by the name of Jack Brown.
I also learned that the City Police were on constant watch
for me, I have, as you see, cut the article from the paper in
which I found it, and now show it to you.

Finding that Cincinnati was not a safe place for me, I
went secretly and set the men at work filling up and signing the blank bills. I then left the city, but discovering
that the Sheriffs and Constables back in the country were
also on the alert for Jack Brown, it would have been rash-
ness in the extreme, as I thought, and you will readily acknowledge, for me to have gone back to Indiana.

Under these circumstances I resolved to return through
Columbus, and Berkshire, to meet you and the boys at
Adrian. As soon as they arrive we will take counsel

together, and decide upon the best course to pursue. If necessary, one of the boys must go after Fox.

This explanation, accompanied by the article purporting to have been cut from a Cincinnati daily paper, was a satisfactory explanation to Royce for the absence of Fox. He congratulated me on my fortunate and hair-breadth escape, and expressed the opinion that it would not be necessary to send for Fox to assist in the bank robbery, as from my description of the situation of matters, he judged that four of us would be sufficient to make the raise.

He stated that the name of the old Jereey farmer, who was about to have been robbed by Long and Birch, went by the name of *Wilborne.* He had mistaken the name, when he saw me in Berkshire. The boys upon learning that he had seen *Tom Brown,* and upon being informed of the project for robbing the South Bend Bank, had decided at once in favor of abandoning the *Wilborne Robbery.* He said that they were in high spirits, and full of animation, at the prospect of uniting with their old friend Tom Brown, in an operation of so much promise. They had not seen him since he fled from Nauvoo. at the time the Hodges were arrested.

The afternoon passed away in conversation, and at evening we each returned to our respective hotels, to await the arrival of Long and Birch.

I watched for the approach of the murderers until eleven o'clock at night, and was about to retire, when a messenger arrived from Lower Sandusky, bearing the welcome intelligence of the arrest of Long and Birch at that place, by a posse under the direction of R. Dickinson, Esq.

Sheriff Thrift, at my request immediately arrested Royce, keeping him in total ignorance of the part I was acting in

12

the affair. Nothing was found upon his person of a criminal character, except one ten dollar counterfeit bill, upon the State Bank of Missouri. This was not considered sufficient to hold him to trial on a criminal charge, but at my request he was kept in custody for four days. I desired this, that he might be prevented from conveying the intelligence of the arrest of Long and Birch to their confederates in the Davenport murder, until I could reach Rock Island and secure their arrest.

Upon the person of Royce were also found three pistols, a bowie knife and a bundle of small slips of paper containing names of persons, to the number of three or four hundred, who were supposed to be members of the organized gang of assassins in various parts of the country.

We left Perrysburgh at two o'clock on the morning of the 19th of September, and arriving at Lower Sandusky about six, found Long and Birch safely lodged in jail.

I called upon R. Dickinson, Esq., who had conducted the arrest, from whom I learned the particulars.

About five o'clock in the afternoon of the day on which I had left Lower Sandusky the southern stage arrived, containing two passengers bearing a general resemblance to the description I had given Mr. Dickinson of Long and Birch. He had repaired to the stage house, examined the way bill and found their names entered as Henderson and Blecher. By this time, the two passengers had been taken to the Railroad House. Mr. Dickinson immediately raised a posse, proceeded to the house and arrested the murderers.

An individual of suspicious appearance approached the house in advance of the posse and informed Long and Birch that they were about to be arrested.

At even that moment Birch was standing at the bar, having first called for a glass of liquor. The landlord had stepped out for a pitcher of water.

Birch ran to the door and saw the posse advancing within a few feet of him. He turned his back to them and tore from his watch the gold chain which he had taken from Col. Davenport, at the time of his murder, threw it inside of the bar, and turned again towards the door, when the posse rushed in and seized him.

A more full account was afterwards given me by B. J. Bartlett and C. K. Watson, Esq., Attorney at Law at Lower Sandusky, who aided in the arrest.

Mr. Bartlett and Mr. Pease took Birch by the arms, and Mr. Dickinson demanding to see his watch, drew it from his pocket, exclaiming:

" This is the watch!"

Birch said: " That is not his watch, it is my watch."

Messrs. Pease and Bartlett then conducted Birch to the court house, while others did the same by Long. On arriving there they were placed in separate rooms, and Bartlett commenced searching Birch. He found eight dollars in paper money, a little silver, a box of percussion caps, bullets, bowie-knife, a gold breast-pin, a gold lever watch, and shortly after a gold chain and seal were brought in, said to have been found near the place of arrest. This chain had been so forcibly detached from the watch, that the gold ring connecting them, was straightened out.

Birch refused to give any account of himself, and declined answering all questions.

Long also adopted the same course of conduct. Neither of them was informed that they were arrested on a charge of murder.

Mr. Watson's statement was similar to that of Bartlett. He gave the name of the man who had apprised Birch of his danger, as Nelson Rich. Upon the person of John Long was found a silver watch, and a few memoranda.

When I first entered the jail at Lower Sandusky, where Long and Birch were confined, Long inquired of me for what murder they were arrested.

"For the murder of Colonel Davenport, of Rock Island," I replied.

"Rock Island!" said he, as if he had never before heard the name. "Rock Island, where is that place? I never was there. I don't know of any such place. I thought we were arrested on charge of having committed the Xenia murder, in Ohio."

This murder alluded to by Long occurred about the 3d of August. A store was broken open, two clerks who were sleeping in it, murdered, and the building robbed, and set on fire.

Before leaving the jail Long tried by offering bribes, to induce me to let him escape.

"It is of no use, Long, to make such an attempt upon me."

"What are you going to do with us?"

"Take you to Rock Island."

"To be hung, I suppose."

"Yes, if you are convicted by a jury of your country-men."

"By ——! you will lose your own life before you get me there."

"I shall run my risk of that."

"I have lots of friends all along the road, who will

avenge any injury done to me. You had better accept my offer and let me escape."

" Long," I replied, " I am neither to be bribed by your promises nor intimidated by your threats. You stand arrested on a charge of having committed a high crime. As to your guilt or innocence, it is not for me to inquire. My duty as an officer, requires me to convey you safely to Rock Island and deliver you both up to the proper authorities, and if I live, I shall do it."

Sheriff Thrift and myself spent the remainder of the day in seeing that the prisoners were properly ironed, preparatory to our starting on our journey with them.

On the morning of the 20th, we left Lower Sandusky by stage for Detroit, reaching that place on the following day. We lodged the prisoners in jail, for safe keeping over night. The next morning we took them on board of the cars for St. Joseph, Michigan.

As the cars were about leaving Detroit, the jailor took me one side and informed me that Long had met with an old confederate in prison, and had told him that I would never succeed in getting them through to Rock Island. That he and Birch intended to watch for an opportunity to get hold of our pistols, kill us, and make their escape. If they could not succeed in this, they had friends enough in Chicago, and between Chicago and Rock Island, who would find some means to rescue them, and set them at liberty.

I communicated this information to Sheriff Thrift, and placed Birch under his immediate custody, taking Long under my own, as I believed him to be the boldest and most desperate of the two.

After traveling a considerable distance, Long finding himself closely guarded, and that his chance of getting hold of my pistols was not good, interrogated me as to the cause of suspicion having been fixed upon them, but getting no satisfactory answer, broke out upon me with all the violence of his nature.

"Bonney! I tell you, you have got into a ——— tight place. Birch has a great many friends in the country we are about to pass through, and they will have their revenge for this arrest. If *he* is injured, *you* will suffer the consequences—mark my words!"

These remarks, added to his threats in the jail at Lower Sandusky, and a disclosure of his desperate plans and intentions towards myself and Sheriff Thrift, induced me to deal harshly with him.

"Long," said I, "you must make no more threats, nor attempt to escape. If you do either, I will put a hundred weight of iron on you. I will hoop you from head to foot. If I see you trying to escape, you are a dead man: mark *my* words! Neither flatter yourself that your friends will rescue you from my custody. They can never take you away alive. I intend to treat you well, but I shall keep you safe. Believe me when I tell you that you and Birch *must* go to Rock Island, dead or alive."

This decided reply seemed to have the desired effect upon Long. He was sullen and restless for a few hours, after which he gave me no more trouble.

Birch afterwards made another attempt to bribe me, by offering a large sum of money, saying, that if I would suffer them to escape, he could readily command ten thousand dollars, through the assistance of his friends, which sum he would secure to me.

I replied that I was acting in the discharge of an official duty, and that I had no price, except to fulfil the obligations resting upon me.

"Very well, sir," said he, "if my offer is unavailing, will you tell me what course you shall pursue, if my friends attempt to rescue us?"

"I shall shoot you both. You may consider that the moment such an attempt is made, is the last moment of your existence."

"But you would not kill *us*, we are ironed and can do nothing. We would not be to blame."

"I know very well, Birch, that none of your friends will attempt your rescue, without some previous sign from you. You *must* go to Rock Island. Your only chance for escape is from the legal tribunals of the land. If you want to get there alive, you must give your friends no signal to interfere with me, whilst I am in the discharge of my duty."

From Detroit we reached Marshal by railroad, at the dusk of evening. We then took stage for St. Joseph, which we reached late in the afternoon of the next day, and embarked on board the steamer Champion, bound for Chicago. In consequence of a heavy gale upon the lake, the Champion was compelled to remain at St. Joseph until the evening of the 24th, during which time Captain E. B. Ward rendered us all the assistance in his power.

While on our passage from St. Joseph to Chicago, Birch was exceedingly restless and frequently complained of sickness.

Sheriff Thrift was constantly with him, permitting him to go wherever he chose upon the deck of the boat. When within a few miles of Chicago, Birch and Thrift passed into the gentleman's cabin where I was keeping watch over Long. Thrift seated himself in a chair, and exhausted by constant watching and fatigue, soon fell into a sound sleep.

Birch perceiving that the sheriff was lost in sleep, started from his seat and moved cautiously towards the companion way. I asked him where he was going? He said that he was sea-sick and wanted to go on deck. Knowing that it was impossible for him to escape from the boat, without jumping overboard, and that as he was heavily ironed, he could not swim for a moment, I suffered him for the first time during the passage to go on deck alone.

In about ten minutes he returned to the cabin, and was speedily followed by the porter of the boat, who informed me that the prisoner had entered the captain's office, where the clerk of the boat was sleeping at the time, and taken from it my portmanteau, which contained my traveling baggage together with all the articles taken from the prisoners at the time of their arrest, except the gold watch and breast pin found upon Birch, and the watch-chain and seal of Col. Davenport. These I had taken the precaution to keep about my person. Birch, after getting the portmanteau had hurriedly thrown it with its contents into the lake.

Among the articles lost with the portmanteau was the silver watch of which the Methodist Minister was robbed. Also the bowie knife that Birch flourished over the head of Mrs. Mulford, and a pistol belonging to John Long, which in all probability was the one from which Colonel Davenport had his fatal wound.

On reaching Chicago, the porter made and subscribed an affidavit before Esq. Kercheval, Justice of the Peace, setting forth the above facts.

Birch afterwards confessed that he threw my portmanteau overboard for the purpose of destroying the evidence of his guilt, supposing it contained the watch-chain and seal of Col. Davenport.

I conveyed the prisoners from the steamboat to the Chicago jail, and placed them in the custody of Sheriff Lowe, until eleven o'clock.

While in jail, Mr. Wentworth of the Chicago Democrat, called to see the prisoners, and informed them of the arrest of Bridge, Oliver and McDole, on Rock River, and also of the disclosures of West.

Birch became much alarmed, cried, and earnestly begged that he might remain confined in Chicago, until the excitement throughout the country should have subsided. He said he was afraid that he should be lynched; that he was a very bad man, was guilty of robbery, larceny, etc., but protested his innocence of the Davenport murder.

Long in the meantime appeared perfectly cool and unconcerned. He said that he had nothing to fear. He had never wronged a man in his life, and

" As for you, Birch, you are a d———d fool, for making such a fuss."

Being myself worn down by constant watchfulness, and having still one hundred and eighty miles to travel through a sparsely populated country, where Long expected assistance from his friends to aid his escape, I considered it only common prudence to put extra irons upon the prisoners. I also employed Deputy Sheriff Wisencraft of Chicago, a vigilant and trustworthy police officer, to accompany me to Rock Island.

Frink, Walker & Co. furnished us with an extra stage coach in which we left Chicago. Unfortunately for our quiet and unmolested passage through the country, the stage left immediately after the arrival of the steamboat Champion, conveying passengers who had been with us crossing the lake, and who spread the news of the arrest of the Davenport murderers, several hours in advance of us, giving the friends of the prisoners sufficient time to rally to their rescue, if they were disposed to hazard the attempt. Orders, however, at our request were sent by the mail stage to the stage agent at Dixon, to detain the stage at that place, until the arrival of the extra. We hoped by this means to prevent the news getting in advance of us, beyond that point.

At Naperville, thirty miles west of Chicago, I met with Hon. Judge Thomas, then holding his court at that place. Judge Thomas, having some knowledge of the extent and power of the gang, in the interior of the country, advised me to leave the main stage road, on the line of which the news had preceded me, and by reaching Dixon on a circuitous route, avoid any concerted interception by the gang.

We however determined to go ahead on the main road, and if molested to cut our way through, if possible, and if overpowered, to put the prisoners to death, rather than allow them to escape their just reward.

We reached Little Rock about midnight, where the drivers made an effort to detain us until morning. After some altercation, however, we compelled them to go on.

We were now approaching the heart of the country most infested by the gang. Although not disturbed by fear, we were watchful and anxious. Not to have felt some degree of doubt, would have been unnatural. There was enough in the scene and place itself to create in our minds a certain degree of anxiety. It was midnight, and our little party was alone, in the midst of an almost boundless prairie. Every turn in the road, every little rise of the prairie, might be the ambuscade of deadly and determined men, ready to hazard their own lives, and reckless of ours, to set their old companions at liberty.

No wonder that we gazed out earnestly upon the moonless night, and were grateful even for the faint star rays which cast a feeble light upon the darkness and desolation of the scene.

We passed on in silence. Nothing was heard but the rumbling wheels, and the heavy breathing of the prisoners.

Each hour of that dreary night seemed almost like an age of ordinary existence; we were ready and determined to resist with desperation any attack which should be made.

After passing a few miles from Little Rock, two men made their appearance on horseback, emerging from a thicket, by the roadside, and came up alongside of the coach. A glass lamp was burning in the coach, and the windows and curtains were closed.

These men attempted to look into the stage, first, by putting their faces against the windows, and then by attempting to lift up the curtains. They seemed desirous of ascertaining our strength. They then fell back, and after apparently holding a consultation, again advanced, and repeated their manœuvre.

At this time, Birch, in a careless way, but evidently to test my determination, said:

" Bonney, these men are our friends. They have come to rescue us, as we told you they would."

I replied promptly, " The moment they make the attempt shall be the last you pass on earth."

"You have a savage disposition, Bonney; would you murder us?"

"I would not call it murder. It would be taking the law in my own hands, and I would not be afraid to meet any court in Christendom on the issue."

Wisencraft gave them the same assurance, and they appeared fully convinced that such would be our action if they were to signal their friends, and accordingly withheld it.

These two men continued to accompany us until near the dawn of day, often approaching the coach, but not once addressing any remark to its occupants, or to the driver. They then left us, and we saw no more of them.

About nine o'clock in the morning we reached Dixon, and found the mail stage awaiting our arrival, to accompany us to Rock Island.

From Dixon we proceeded on our way without interruption, and without noticing anything worthy of suspicion, until we arrived within sixteen miles of Rock Island, where we stopped to take supper.

While we were at supper a stranger took his seat in the extra we had chartered for our transportation, and that of the prisoners, and expressed his determination in opposition to all reasonable entreaties to accompany us as far as Rock Island. He was offered a seat in the regular mail coach, which he refused to aeccpt. I was at length under the necessity of ejecting him by force.

About midnight of the 26th of September we reached Rock Island, and delivered our prisoners into the custody of Lemuel Andrews, Sheriff of Rock Island County, who lodged them safely in jail.

CHAPTER XVI.

BEING myself worn down by fatigue and ill health, I was compelled to remain at Rock Island, and entrust the arrest of the residue of the murderers to other hands.

In less than two hours after my arrival, D. P. Gregg, and Joseph Johnston, of Rock Island, were on their way to arrest Aaron Long who was then residing about six miles east of Galena, and John Baxter, who was then in Wisconsin, near Jefferson City.

Birch finding himself safely lodged in jail, with no hope of escape, and the prospect of a speedy trial, intimated his willingness to make some disclosures, which might aid the authorities in a further prosecution of the gang, and lead to a recovery of the lost money and watch.

I accordingly took Birch from his cell, and conducted him to a room in the jailor's dwelling, where he commenced a confession, which he completed the following day. In his confession it will be noticed that Birch cautiously works himself out of the scrape, by endeavoring to account for his absence, and substituting the name of *Brown* in his stead, to make out the number. At a subsequent confession he so far contradicted his first one, as to admit that he was a participator in the robbery and murder of Col. Davenport, with a personal knowledge of the whole affair.

The substance of his confession was as follows:

Confession of Robert Birch at Rock Island.—About the 27th of last June, John Long, Aaron Long, William Fox and myself, left Fort Madison, in Iowa Territory, in company, on the steamboat Osprey. We went up the Mississippi, passed Rock Island, and landed at New Albany. Then all of us went up into the woods back from the river, eight or nine miles. John Long and myself went to a Mr. Miller's, who was said to have a large amount of money. We both passed the house, and observed carefully the situation of it. I passed on alone a short distance, while John went on to meet Aaron Long and Fox.

Fox went to Miller's and staid over night. In the morning he asked Miller to change a ten dollar bill. This was for the purpose of ascertaining where Miller kept his money. Miller not being able to change the bill, we concluded he had not much money by him, and his robbery was abandoned for a while.

Fox and the Longs went from there to Fulton, where they met with a man calling his name *Lee*, or *Little Brown.*

I went over to Rock River, to help Bridge break jail.

Fox, John, Aaron and Brown, stole a skiff and went down the river to a place near Rock Island, where they camped out. They remained there for several days, until the 4th of July. On that day they crossed the slough on to the Island in the same skiff they had stolen up the river. They had previously ascertained that the family of Col. Davenport would all be absent from the Island.

Fox and John Long entered the house of Col. Davenport through a back window, and commenced searching the house for money, leaving Aaron outside of the door to keep watch.

As they were passing through a back hall, and about to enter into the parlor, Col. Davenport came into the room from another door. Fox turned to fly, when John Long cried to him:

" *Take him, Chunky!*"

Fox turning, drew a pistol, and said to Davenport:

"Stand, sir!"

At this instant, the pistol went off accidentally, and shot Davenport through the thigh.

They then tied him, blindfolded him with Fox's red silk handkerchief, and taking him up stairs, made him unlock his safe, and after robbing it, they left Davenport on the bed, with a pitcher of water standing within his reach. They told me afterwards that they took from Davenport exactly four hundred dollars in notes, one five france piece, his gold watch and chain, a gun, and one pistol.

John Long said that when they left the house, he was afraid that the old man would die, he bled so freely, and had fainted two or three times.

They then re-crossed the slough, and fled to Rock River, where they stole another skiff, passed down the stream a few miles, and landed on the opposite shore. They proceeded on to New Boston, stole another skiff, and floated down the Mississippi to Nauvoo. From there they went over to Old Redden's at Devil Creek, and secreted the money and watch which they had taken from Davenport in Old Redden's wheat field.

John Baxter is the man who informed them of the particulars which induced them to assail Col. Davenport. He is the man who got up the sight. By this term, I mean that he planned and arranged the robbery. He was not on the Island at the time it took place, but he advised and gave all necessary intelligence in the matter.

Fox was the man who robbed Knox & Drury's office at Rock Island. He got about six hundred dollars. Baxter also planned *that* robbery, and told Fox where to find the money. This was previous to the robbery of Col. Davenport. When Fox returned from accomplishing it, I was boarding with Loomis at Nauvoo. Fox arrived there in the night time after I had retired to bed. The next morning Loomis told me that he had got back, and had made a pretty good raise. He said he would be in again in the evening. That night Fox and myself slept together, and held a long consultation. He said he had the best sight on Rock Island he had ever found in his life. It was to rob old Col. Davenport, who had over one hundred thousand dollars in his house, and that John Baxter who knew all about Davenport's circumstances, would give him all the information he wanted, whenever he got ready to do the job. It would be enough to make them all rich, and then they would quit the business.

After the boys had robbed Davenport, and I returned from Rock River, I met John, Aaron and Fox, at old Grant Redden's, on Devil Creek.

Aaron Long and William H. Redden went to Nauvoo, about the 12th of July, and there heard that Davenport was dead, and saw an advertisement for the murderers, describing the watch, and a part of the money. It also contained a partial description of the perpetrators of the deed.

Aaron Long returned to Redden's, told Fox, John and myself the news, and said that the description of two of the murderers was a d——d good one of John and Fox.

The same night John and Fox went out into Old Redden's wheat field, took up the money and watch which they had got from Davenport, and then took the gun and pistol and went a considerable distance upon the prairie, and secreted them.

The money was then divided in Redden's house, Aaron Long receiving one hundred and forty dollars for his share.

Aaron then left Redden's and went back into Iowa Territory to steal a horse, after which he was to return to his father's, near Galena.

Fox, John, and I started for Missouri, and traveled till towards morning, when we crept into a large thicket, and slept till after sunrise. We then traveled on until within one or two miles of the Des Moines River, when we stopped at a farm house and got breakfast. Here John purchased some beeswax, telling the woman of the house that he was a tailor by trade, and was about to settle in his business at Farmington, about eight or ten miles distant.

After getting breakfast, we left the main road, passed down a ravine back of the house, and at a distance of about a half mile, stopped, and made preparations to conceal the money and watch. They told me to take the beeswax and lay it on a rock to warm in the sun. A portion of the paper money taken from Knox and Dewey, was put into a glass bottle, together with some money that Fox, Long and others, had taken from a man by the name of Strawn, in Putnam County, Illinois. This bottle containing some eight or nine hundred dollars, was sealed over with beeswax, and buried near that place, together with about two hundred dollars in silver tied up in a cloth. Davenport watch was also enclosed in beeswax to prevent injury from wet, and buried with the money. When all had been got

13

in readiness for the burial, Fox passed on a short distance up the bluff, and buried it.

We then traveled on in company, crossed the Des Moines River, at an old mill, six or eight miles below Farmington, and went back into Macon County, Missouri, where Fox and Long stopped, while I went on ten or twelve miles farther to see a man by the name of Moat. I desired to ascertain from this Moat, where a certain race mare was kept, belonging to a Mr. Inyard, who, I knew, lived somewhere in the neighborhood of Centreville, Missouri. I obtained the desired information, and returning, told Fox and Long. Long stole the mare the following night. Fox and I stole two horses fifteen miles from Centreville, on the Glasgow road, and took them with the race mare to St. Louis. We left the two horses with Reynolds at St. Louis, and crossed the Mississippi, to Illinois Town, about the first of August. The next night we stole three horses at Belleville, then traveled east, crossing the Wabash river below Terre Haute. From thence we went to Old Mother Long's in Owen County, Indiana. These three horses and the race mare, were the same animals found in the possession of Fox, at the time he was arrested and put in jail, at Bowling Green, in Clay County, Indiana.

This information received from Birch in his confession, in addition to that already derived from Granville Young, clearly confirmed the guilt of John Baxter. N. Belcher, Esq., on the following day left Rock Island for Wisconsin, to aid Gregg and Johnson in the arrest of Baxter.

On the same day I received intelligence of the escape of Fox from the custody of T. B. Johnson at Indianapolis, on the 16th day of September. Upon a full examination of the facts and circumstances connected with this escape, I

am satisfied in my own mind that Johnson was bribed by
Fox. To say the least of it, he was guilty of gross neglect
and culpable misconduct. He violated every pledge he had
made me, relative to the manner of keeping Fox. He
never confined him in jail, as he was instructed to do, but
kept him from the time of his arrival at Indianapolis, until
he effected his escape, a period of eight days, in an upper
room of Browning's Hotel, and placed no other irons upon
him than a pair of light handcuffs.

George L. Davenport was absent from home at St. Louis,
at the time of my arrival at Rock Island. On his return
he called at Fort Madison, and learned that a gun and
pistol had been found near old Grant Redden's, secreted in
the grass, at the edge of a slough on the prairie, the description of which answered to that of his father's. He
went the distance of eight miles for the purpose of seeing
them, and recognized them at once. He reached home
with them a few days after the confession of Birch, thus far
confirming his statements. This becoming publicly known,
re-awakened the animosity of the people against the Redden's. The inhabitants of Lee County determined to submit no longer to the depredations of the gang, and eager to
investigate every suspicious circumstance, and ferret out the
truth, they raised a posse at Fort Madison, to go and arrest
the Reddens, and search their premises for stolen property.

Sheriff Estes, being familiar with my plans and proposed
movements, opposed the arrest of the Reddens, fearing
that it might prevent the capture of the principal murderers.
At that time he had not heard of the arrest of Fox, John
Long and Birch. The posse however proceeded to the
house of Redden, seized the old man, his son William H.
Redden, and Granville Young, and lodged them all in jail,

at Fort Madison. The Reddens were retained there, but Young was soon afterwards removed to Rock Island, on suspicion of being engaged in the Davenport murder.

From the description received from Birch of the concealment of the money, on the Des Moines River, and, from the account given me by Reynolds, at St. Louis, and from information derived from Fox himself, Deputy Sheriff Cob of Rock Island, and myself took Birch from jail to assist us in searching for it. Accompanied by Wisencraft, and joined at Fort Madison by Sheriff Estes, and others of Lee County, we started under the direction of Birch for the spot where Fox had left him, to bury the money. We found everything exactly as described by him, the house where they had taken breakfast, the woman who sold Long the beeswax, the ravine, the old mill, the place where Fox overtook Birch after burying the money, but failed to find the money itself. After making diligent search we took our way back to Rock Island. Birch felt much disheartened at our want of success, thinking that it would be still worse for him, after having put us to so much trouble for nothing. He was now in a state of utter despair, and believed the evidence against him sufficient to prove his guilt. The Circuit Court would be held at Rock Island the following week, and he expected to be tried, condemned, and executed without further delay. He therefore considered that it would be useless for him longer to protest his innocence of the murder, and made another confession to Sheriff Estes, which was as follows:

Confession of Birch to Estes.—I was present when Col. Davenport was murdered, in company with Fox, John Long and Aaron Long. *John Long was the man who shot Davenport*, but the shot was accidental. There was some defect in the lock of the pistol, and when John cocked it, it went off, hitting the old man in the knee or thigh, We did not choke and abuse the old man, as represented, but frequently wet his face with cold water, as he bled pro-fusely, and fainted several times from loss of blood. We wanted to keep him alive, to make him tell where his money was.

Before we left the house, the boys wanted to kill the old man, but I opposed it. I never believed in killing. I would willingly have staid and taken care of the old Colonel all night, if I had dared to have done so.

I intend to write a book, and tell everything I know about the whole gang. I expect to be hanged, and I want to do the world all the good I can before I die. I know a great many things about the boys who were engaged in this kind of business, and I wish to tell it all."

As I was about leaving Fort Madison, on my return to Rock Island with Birch, the Reddens, who had been till this time confined in jail at Fort Madison, were ordered before Judge Mason at Burlington, Iowa, on a writ of Habeas Corpus.

Sheriff Estes took them on the same boat to convey them to Burlington, on which I had embarked for Rock Island.

The steamboat arrived at Burlington, twenty-four miles from Fort Madison about twelve o'clock at night. Estes landed and went in pursuit of the jailor at Burlington, to take his prisoners in custody for safe keeping until morning, leaving the prisoners (the Reddens,) in the care of T. A. Walker, who had accompanied him as assistant. While Estes was off on the mission after the jailor, the steamboat left the landing with the prisoners and guards and arrived at Rock Island the following day, where they were immediately taken into custody by the Sheriff of Rock Island County, on charge of aiding in the murder of Col. Davenport. During my absence, Doct. Gregg, James Johnson and N. Belcher had returned with Baxter and Aaron Long, and had them safely lodged in prison.

The October term of the Rock Island Circuit Court, being already in session, John Baxter, William Fox, John Long, Aaron Long, Robert H. Birch, Granville Young, Grant Redden and Wm. H. Redden were severally indicted as principals and accessories in the murder of Col. Davenport, of Rock Island County.

Further confessions of Birch, were in substance as follows:

" The first council for arranging the robbery of Col. Davenport was held in Joseph Smith's old council chamber in Nauvoo.

" Fox, John and Aaron Long, Jack Redden, and Hodges, O. P. Rockwell, John Ray, Wm. Louther, myself and several others whose names I don't now recollect were present. I told the boys I was opposed to robbing Davenport, as I had been at Rock Island several weeks during the winter previous, for the purpose of ascertaining whether Davenport kept any considerable amount of money by him. I became satisfied by good authority, that if we should attempt to rob him we should not raise more than one thousand or fifteen hundred dollars, as I was informed he kept his money in banks, which would not be enough to pay for the risk, as I was satisfied it would be a difficult and dangerous operation to get the old man's money, and get away safe with it. The boys disagreed with me. Fox said Baxter had lived with Davenport, and knew all about his circumstances, and had told him they would get as much as thirty or forty thousand dollars. They all thought that Baxter knew better about Davenport's circumstances than I did, and thought it best to rake the old fellow down.

"Rockwell remarked, that it was best for us to monopolize the business, as there was enough of us to raise all the good sights we could find.

"Fox and myself attempted to rob Beach in Nauvoo, and would have succeeded, had not Brigham Young told Beach the plan. We came near being caught, but escaped, and crossed the river to Old Redden's.

"When we left Redden's to go up and rake down Old Davenport, we met with Young, and Bundy, at Fort Madison. I had never seen Young before, but Long and Fox were well acquainted with him, and told him where we were going. Young wanted to go with us. The boys introduced us to each other, and told me that he wanted to join us, and were in favor of allowing him to do so. I did not like his looks, and said to the boys that I would not have him with us. I thought he was a d———d suspicious looking fellow, and that it was not safe to trust him, and as we had been at considerable trouble and expense in getting up the sight, that we might as well have the whole benefit of the raise among ourselves, as make a further division of it, by admitting another partner.

"Young did not accompany us from Forst Madison, but went somewhere up the river to sell a couple of horses he said he had stolen over on the Illinois river.

Aaron Long took no part in the murder of Col. Davenport, he being left out of doors to keep watch.

"If you want to arrest Fox, I can tell you where to find him. He and Tom Brown are together, either at Adrian, or at Niles, in Michigan, not far from South Bend. If you start soon you will find him at one of those places, and I hope you will succeed in arresting him, for if we are to have a fuss, we may as well all take our chances together. Tom Brown and Artemas Johnson were both concerned with Stephen and William Hodges in the murder of Miller and Liecy.

" Fox and John Baker robbed the peddler at Troy Grove —the most of the goods were taken to Nauvoo and secreted with Doctor A. B. Williams, and afterwards taken to Packard's Grove, where Baker remained to sell the goods, and Fox went South to spend the winter. Williams received a share of the goods for his trouble in secreting them."

Up to the time of this confession Birch was ignorant of the plot by which he and John Long had been entrapped, and of the arrest of Fox. He supposed that Fox was with Royce and Tom Brown, (the name I had assumed,) near Adrian, waiting to rob the South Bend Bank.

Soon afterwards, however, the jailor at Rock Island, disclosed to them, the whole plot by which they had been pursued and arrested, and that the person who had been traveling in the gang for several months under the name of Tom Brown, who they supposed was Tom Brown of Nauvoo, was no other than Bonney. This information spread with the rapidity of lightning to all parts of the gang. Much terror and confusion was created by it, as their future safety depended on my destruction, as by my successful stratagem, I had obtained an extensive knowledge of their operations. All their exertions therefore were immediately brought to bear to accomplish this purpose.

The disclosures of Birch led to an attempt to arrest Jack Redden, as accessory to the murder of Col. Davenport. L

E. Johnson was deputied to make the arrest, under authority of a warrant issued by Miles W. Conway, Esq., Justice of the Peace.

Johnson repaired to Nauvoo, accompanied by Mr. Bradley of Burlington, Iowa. In attempting to make this arrest, these gentlemen were attacked by a large number of the Mormon gang, friendly to Redden, and after being severely beaten and wounded, were compelled to abandon the attempt. Mob law was triumphant, and the arm of the law of the land utterly powerless.

CHAPTER XVII.

TRIAL OF GRANVILLE YOUNG AND THE TWO LONGS.

THE regular session of the Rock Island Circuit Court commenced on the 6th day of October, 1845, His Honor, Judge Brown, presiding. T. J. Turner, Esq., State's Attorney.

The same day, the Grand Jury found bills of indictment against Birch, Fox, the two Longs, Baxter and Young, for the murder of Col. George Davenport. Baxter was remanded to jail, and Young and the two Longs put upon trial.

A large number of jurymen were challenged for cause, and a few peremptorily. It was not till Thursday that a full jury was sworn.

The case for the prosecution was opened by Mr. Mitchell.

Mr. Wilkinson opened for the prisoners. The first witness introduced by the prosecution was Dr. P. Gregg, who being sworn, said:

" I am a physician and surgeon. On the 4th day of July last, I was summoned to attend at the house of Col. Davenport. Upon arriving there I found Doctors Witherwax and Brown, up stairs with the Colonel, who was lying on the bed, with a gun-shot wound in his left thigh. On examination, it was decided that the wound required no

great attention. The Colonel was sinking fast, from ex-
haustion, in great agony, and cold from head to foot. I
examined the wound, and found that there had been a
profuse flow of blood. The blood was *everywhere.* The
house looked like a butcher's shamble—blood in the sitting-
room, in the hall, and along up the stairs, and in the closet
by the safe was a pool of blood, and in the room below
there was the same. On the door case of the closet containing the safe, was the mark of a bloody hand. The left
left leg of his pantaloons and the bed clothes were saturated
with blood. I observed a contusion on his left arm or side,
and he appeared as if he had been bruised or beaten. The
gun-shot wound, and bad treatment killed him. I am of
the opinion that any man of his age, without assistance,
would have died of the gun-shot wound. He was shot that
day. I heard his dying declarations. He said he expected
to die, and was not afraid. Said he was sitting in his front
room, when hearing a noise in the back part of the house,
he fancied it was some one at the well after water. The
noise continuing, he arose to go and see what it was, when
he was instantly assailed by three or more men. One of
them shot him through the thigh, and these all rushed
upon him, threw him down, bound and blindfolded him.
The robbers forced him up stairs, dragging him by the
neck to the closet, where his iron safe was placed, and being
unable to open it themselves, compelled him to do so. They
then forced him into his bed in another room, and choked
him until he was almost dead.

" His whole body was cold, and he entreated continually
for something to ease him, and while we were rubbing his
wounded leg, he would still call on us to rub it.

" After the robbers had placed him on the bed, they inquired for more money. He told them that there was money in the bureau. On examining it, they mistook the drawer, and found no money, upon which they choked him until he was nearly senseless. They made him drink water, and threw it upon him, to bring him to again. One of the robbers was a short, slim man, to whom the Colonel made frequent allusion.

" The Colonel died that day; I was with him at the time."

Cross Examined.—The Colonel seemed to know that he was in a dying condition; I endeavored to encourage him, but could not efface the impression. He said they rushed on him, bandaged his eyes, and tied his arms and legs.

Examination in chief resumed.—He stated that the men got between six and seven hundred dollars in gold, silver, and Missouri bank notes, with his gold watch and chain.

Benjamin Cole.—I was out on the 4th day of July fishing until the middle of the day. I went down the river to Rock Island or Davenport. There were two men and a boy in the skiff with me. As we came opposite to Col. Davenport's house, between one and two o'clock, I heard the cry of *Murder! Help! For God's sake:*

When I said to those who were with me, that some one was in distress there, and I would go and see about it, they remarked that it was probably only a piece of sport, as it was the 4th of July. Hearing the cry again, I declared I would go and see at any rate. We accordingly rowed to the shore, and went up to the house. At the gate, I wa' met by a large bull dog and was obliged to coax hir a while, before he would allow me to pass. I rapped at the door, but no one answered. I opened it, and the first thing

I saw was a puddle of blood. I went to the back part of
the house, but could neither hear nor see any one. I then
went into the hall, from whence I heard the Colonel up
stairs, calling for me to come up there. I went up instantly,
and found him lying on the bed. He asked me why I did
not come sooner. I replied that I had come as soon as
possible, and was ready to do anything for him. He desired
me to go for Doctor Brown, who he said was near the
house, being in attendance at a pic-nic party, on the Island.
I told the men to stay, and I ran for the Doctor. On my
return, I sent the news to Davenport and Rock Island.
Doctor Brown and myself watched the Colonel, and found
the wound, which had nearly done bleeding. He said that
a gang of robbers had broken into his house, taken all his
money, and murdered him.

Cross Examined.—The Colonel said that one of the
gang was a small sized man. He shot him, and then they
jumped on him. The handkerchief was off his head, and
on the bed; he said he was dying.

Robert Birch sworn.—John Long told me that he and
his brother Aaron, and Fox, and Lee or Little Brown had
been at Rock Island, and robbed Old Colonel Davenport.
They had accidentally shot him.

Birch's evidence on this trial, was almost word for word
like his *first* confession.

He said that no inducement had been held out to him to
testify, but he gave his evidence voluntarily.

George L. Davenport sworn.—On the 4th of July last, I
went to my father's house on the Island, in company with
Doctor Gregg. I found my father suffering, in extreme
pain. He told me he had been robbed and murdered. That
three persons had attacked him, one of whom had shot him.

They had bound him, dragged him up stairs by the shirt collar, and choked him nearly to death, to make him disclose where his money was concealed. The man who shot him had on a cloth cap, and was a small, slim man. They told him they would burn the house, and him in it, if he did not disclose where his money was, but the one who shot him opposed this course. They were disturbed, and left him preciptately. The room in which my father was left, overlooked the river. He died about nine o'clock that night.

I got father's gun and pistol about nine miles below Fort Madison, at a Mr. Hopkins. They were found in a slough near by. I had no difficulty in identifying them. The gun had a Dutch name on it, silver pegs, and a split on the side of the stock.

He also identified the watch-chain and seal as having belonged to his father.

Cross Examined.—Father said that they fired at him, and that he rushed for his cane. They followed him and bandaged his eyes. He saw three men, and thought there were more of them. The withes were not on him when I first saw him. He had gnawed them off before he got any assistance, with his teeth. He complained of shortness of breath. His tongue, lips and throat were swollen.

Bailey Davenport sworn.—The statements of this witness are a repetition of his father's dying account of his assassination.

Frederick Redenburgh sworn.—I was a clerk in Belcher's grocery. Aaron Long came in and bought bread of me, a day or two before the 4th of July. I have no doubt of his identity. I saw him on the steamboat in the custody of Gregg and Johnson. He asked for the bread in a hurried manner, paid for it and went out. I do not recognize the other prisoners. Aaron Long bought bread before the 4th of July, not after.

John Long was brought before the ury, and his boots were examined. They were rights and lefts, with small heels.

Mr. Cole recalled.—I saw tracks under the window. John Long's boots look like the same by which the small tracks were made.

Dr. Gregg recalled.—I measured the track under the window at Col. Davenport's house, and at Wilson's Ferry, on Rock River, and found them identical.

William Kale sworn.—I recognize John Long. I saw him at the saloon in Rock Island, the week of the 4th of July. He bought some liquor, and had it put in a pint flask. The first time he was there he staid but a short time, and went up the river towards Moline. He was also at the saloon, and bought liquor on the morning of the 4th of July.

Daniel Stephens sworn.—I found a fine skiff with hickory bark in it up the slough, opposite the Island, about half past four o'clock the 4th of July. The skiff was drawn up out of the river, opposite where the tracks led from Col. Davenport's house to the slough. There were tracks which led up the bank from the skiff towards the bluff. There was one piece of dry bark in the skiff, and one piece of green.

Pieces of bark were shown to the witness, which he swore were the same as those found in the skiff. No owner had ever come for the skiff.

J. B. Cobb sworn.—I remember having seen one of the prisoners, John Long. I was coming from Moline in company with Sheriff Andrews. We met him about opposite to Rock Island. We noticed him more particularly as he had a pistol sticking out of his pantaloons pocket.

William Fuller sworn.—Had seen all three of the prisoners in Iowa, Long went by the name of Henderson.

Frazier Wilson sworn.—I examined the tracks on the 4th of July, leading to the slough, and in several other places. There were three or four distinctly different tracks, one, that of a large square-toed boot, another of a small boot, with a fine round heel. It seemed as if the persons who made them were going rapidly, the heels struck hard, making a deep impression. I also saw the tracks at E. W. Wilson's Ferry on Rock River. They were the same. There were three different tracks on one trail.

Grant Redden sworn.—I know the prisoners, John and Aaron Long, and Granville Young. They were at my house in Lee County, Iowa. John and Aaron were there the 6th or 8th of July. They said they had been to Missouri. I think John Long staid with me all night, but am not certain. Aaron Long staid two nights. I never heard any conversation in relation to Rock Island or Col. Davenport.

Joseph Johnson sworn.—I assisted in arresting Aaron Long, a week ago last Sunday, eight or nine miles from Galena, on Sand Prairie. He was at work, haying. We took him to his father's and searched the old man's house. We found several letters, one written by a Capt. Short. Aaron said he had passed Rock Island several times, but had never stopped there. He wanted to know what he was arrested for. He said he could not imagine unless it was for the murder of Colonel Davenport, or for passing counterfeit money. If for the first, he was innocent. I told him that there was considerable evidence against him. He wanted to know if he could not be sent to the Penitentiary.

While searching Old Long's house we discovered a good many things. A large quantity of calico, linen, table cloths, women's dresses, and also a pair of bloody pants. Aaron said they were his. He said he got them bloodied butchering. Dr. Gregg found them in the bottom of an old box, under other things. We found more than twenty pairs of pantaloons of various sizes, old and new; but only one bloody pair.

I communicated nothing directly to Aaron as to the charge upon which he was arrested, until after he told me that he did not know for what he could have been arrested.

Jesse Maxwell sworn.—I found two coats on the 8th of August, about one hundred and fifty rods to the right of the road leading from here to Moline, in a thicket near the slough. It was about opposite Rock Island. Bushes and leaves were thrown over the coats. Blood was on the sleeves and skirts, a pair of kid gloves in the pocket of one coat.

The gloves were produced and found to resemble a pair in the possession of John Long. The coats were also produced.

Nathaniel Belcher sworn.—The evidence of this witness related to a conversation with Aaron Long in person, in which Long stated repeatedly that he had never been at Rock Island.

David Kirkpatrick sworn.—I was confined in the debtor's prison. Overheard several conversations between John Long and Young before Aaron had been arrested. They said Jack Redden would "shoot."

Young said: "We shall all be hanged."

14*

John Long said: "He was afraid that cowardly Birch would play the devil with them."

I heard no admissions that they were guilty. Young said: "If Jack Redden is caught he will squeal like a pig."

Eston C. Cropper sworn.—I have been keeper of the prisoners. Have overheard a great deal of conversation amongst them. They said Bonney would be "nepoed," which I understand to be their usual phrase for killed. They used the expression "*nepo*" seven or eight times. A good deal of their talk was blind, and I could not understand it.

Dr. H. Brown sworn.—This witness corroborated the statement of others who had described the wounds of Col. Davenport. Those wounds undoubtedly caused his death.

E. Bonney sworn.—The testimony of this witness would be a mere repetition of facts previously stated in the narrative. He refused on his cross-examination, to state the means by which he had ferreted out the robbers, by which he gained the confidence of the gang, giving as his reason, that there were others yet to be arrested.

T. A. Walker sworn.—I was present at the arrest of Young, and that of Old Redden and his son. It was at Redden's house at Devil Creek. We searched the house. Young said he was at Prairie La Porte, on the 4th of July, and had never known Long or Birch. I took particular charge of Young on our way to Fort Madison. He seemed much terrified, and made many contradictory statements. I became convinced that he was connected with the murder of Davenport.

The prosecution here rested the case, and the counsel for the prisoners did the same, having no witnesses to produce.

It is unnecessary to give the arguments of the counsel,

involving, as they did, a constant repetition of the evidence.

Mr. Mitchell opened for the prosecution in a clear, brief speech.

Mr. S. S. Yager for the defence, attended to the fact that the prisoners were denied separate trials, that age and ability had been brought to bear against them. Youth and inexperience employed in their defence. He protested against any credit being given to the evidence of Birch— who was stained with crime, etc., etc. He thought that *Granville Young* assuredly could not be found guilty.

Thomas T. Turner spoke at length for the prosecution; Mr. Cornwall for the defence; and Mr. Joseph Knox closed for the prosecution.

The court informed the jury that they were judges both of the law and fact, and they retired.

After one hour's consultation, they returned a verdict of guilty against John Long, Aaron Long and Granville Young.

The following morning they were brought in for sentence. John Long, true to the last to his daring character, upon hearing his condemnation, bowed gracefully to the judge, and thanked him, as if receiving a favor. The three prisoners were sentenced to be hung on the 19th day of October instant.

The prisoners would no doubt have made a free and true confession of their guilt after their trial and conviction, but for the movements of the gang to suppress it, and at the same time destroy any further efforts on my part to bring others of their number to justice.

Soon after the trial and sentence of the Longs and Young, S. Height, of Keokuk, Iowa Territory, made his appearance at the jail in Rock Island, and was permitted to have an interview with the prisoners. He met them on the most friendly terms of intimacy, extended to them the hand of fellowship, as an old acquaintance, and told them that if they would follow his counsel, he could save them from their impending doom.

As desperate men, they would of course resoit to any measures to effect their escape, and the following conspiracy was agreed upon. Height proceeded at once to Fort Madison, Iowa, where the Grand Jury was then in session, and having procured several of the gang from Nauvoo, took them before the Grand Jury, and upon their oaths, four indictments were procured against me. Three of them were on charge of counterfeiting. The fourth was on charge of the murder of Miller and Liecy, for which the Hodges were executed. An arrest under this charge would prevent me from obtaining bail, and of course I would have to submit to close confinement. With these several indictments he obtained a requisition from Gov. Chambers, of Iowa, on Gov. Ford, of Illinois, intending to have me arrested on the day set for the execution of the Longs and Young.

In the meantime he intended to make such representations to Governor Ford, as would induce him to order reprieves of the murderers, which would give them hopes of a new trial, or of an opportunity to effect their escape from jail through the assistance of their friends in the gang.

In view of my contemplated arrest, and the suspension of their execution through executive interference, and also to excite the public mind against me, the prisoners were to protest their innocence on the scaffold. They were also to charge me with having committed the worst of crimes while addressing the assemblage.

The officer bearing a writ from the Governor for my arrest should then present himself, and take me into custody, all which, would of course, if effectually carried out, create a tremendous excitement against me, and in favor of the prisoners, and might result in a successful attempt to rescue the convicts from the custody of the officers, and enable them to escape.

This plot was well planned, and is a good example of the ingenuity of desperation. The indictments were procured. The requestions were obtained from Governor Chambers, and presented to Governor Ford, who being familiar with my movements to ferret out and arrest the murderers, and being also acquainted with the character of the witnesses upon whose testimony the indictments had been found by the Grand Jury, peremptorily refused to obey the demands of the requisition. He told the messenger that he never would surrender Bonney to the authorities of Iowa, upon any charge made, and attempted to be sustained by such witnesses as those whose names accompanied the requisitions, and immediately addressed a letter to Gov. Chambers, of Iowa, setting forth the facts, and requesting him to recall the requisition.

In the meantime I received a letter from Mr. L. E. Johnson, of Fort Madison, informing me of the indictments which had been found against me, through the influence of Height, Heckman and others, and stating that it was the earnest wish of my friends, who were prepared to sustain me, that I should go down there immediately in advance of the writ.

In accordance with this letter I at once made my preparations to go to Fort Madison. I visited the prisoners in their cells and informed them that I should be absent for several days, and probably should not see them again. Consequently, they were fully aware that I should not be present, on the day of their execution.

Arriving at Fort Madison, I called upon Sheriff Estes, who presented writs issued upon the several indictments, and I surrendered myself into his custody, proposing, as one of the charges was not bailable, that he should commit me to the county prison to await my trial.

After a short pause, the Sheriff said:

"Bonney, this is a hard case! I know the origin of the matter, and the character of the witnesses. I have been familiar with your whole plan of operation to ferret out the gang of robbers, and I will not commit you to prison. No, sir! I will assume a Jacksonian responsibility. I never will turn key upon you. Go where you please! You know what my duty is. If you are in attendance at the next term of the court, it is all that is required of me. Go to your family, or in pursuit of Fox, or where you please."

At my request, Mr. Walker and Mr. Estes wrote to Joseph Knox, Esq., of Rock Island, giving him a full statement of the matter. They informed him that the chief witness against me was *William A. Heckman,* one of the most notorious rascals unhung; a fugitive from justice for several larcenies he had committed in the County of Lee, and who was smuggled into the Grand Jury room without the knowledge of any of the officers of the court. As soon as it was disclosed that he had been before the jury, an effort was made to have him arrested, but he had suddenly disappeared. The Grand Jury would never have found the indictment, if they had not been deceived.

In the meantime the day arrived for the execution of Young and the two Longs. In accordance with the preconcerted arrangement of the muraerers with Height, each of them in turn addressed the crowd.

Young and Aaron Long protested their innocence of the crime, while John Long, doubtless to make himself the hero of the day, confessed his guilt, and exulted in his criminal career. He solemnly protested that Aaron Long and Young were innocent, and charged me with being chief of the gang, and guilty of murder and various other crimes, calling upon me by name, expecting, in accordance with his arrangement with Height, that the officer would come with a writ from the Governor for my arrest. He continued his harangue until the time allowed him had expired and he was stopped by the Sheriff. His last appeal was to his friends for a rescue. He told them he had always been true to them, and to his profession, and his dying request was, that all who called themselves his friends, should " make a port of entry of Bonney's heart."

So sanguine were his hopes of rescue, or of executive interference, that after his cap was drawn over his face, he raised it, and looked off in the direction from which he expected the approach of the messenger. But, alas for the doomed murderer, he looked in vain. An expression of singular despair gathered over his countenance, as the cap again fell, and shut out to him the bright and beautiful world forever. Above him was the clear blue sky of October. Around him the broad brown prairie, and the woods robed in the gorgeous drapery of their glorious autumnal decay. The soft sighing of the wind, the song of birds, the low murmur of the great Mississippi, and the heavy breathings of the indignant crowd of his fellow beings, gathered to witness the fulfilment of the just decree of law, were the last sounds that fell upon his ears as he passed away to "that country from whose bourne no traveler returns."

The drop fell, and the three murderers swung off. John Long and Granville Young were at once launched into eternity. A moment before they were breathing God's air, strong, healthy, young, full of the bounding blood of vigorous life! How narrow the space between life and death! Surely the line of separation between them is so slight, that there must be some strange affinity, could science or philosophy but discover it. The sunbeam hidden by the cloud! The rainbow that melts into ocean! The man that goes down into the grave! Whence come they? and where do they go?

The death of the other murderer was accidentally postponed. His rope broke, and he fell to the ground. He was immediately reconveyed to the scaffold and while the officer was again adjusting the rope, one of the clergymen in attendance, addressed him, saying:

"You see before you the dead bodies of your brother and Young. They have gone, and you must soon follow. You can have no hope of escape! If you are guilty, confess your guilt to God!"

Aaron now for the first time acknowledged his participation in the murder, giving the lie to all his and John's former statements. In another moment he was suspended from the scaffold and his spirit passed to the other world.

There is something repugnant to our feelings in witnessing violent death, even where the victim is deeply stained with crime, and his death demanded and sanctioned by the majesty of law. Such a sight leaves a memory behind that passes not away forever.

John Long was probably one of the most daring villains who ever pursued the career of crime. Of his early history I know nothing more than the reader may glean from the preceding pages. His personal appearance to a casual eye was exccedingly inferior, but to those who scanned him closely, there was an appearance of wonderful activity in his slight but muscular frame, and a bold, determined glance in his dark eyes, that commanded attention. He might never have been a Claude Duval, for he lacked the polish and grace of that most pleasant and accomplished highwayman. He was more like the boisterous and resolute Dick Turpin, equal to every emergency, and bearing his strong heart and high courage even to the gates of death.

So bold was he in falsehood, even on the scaffold, that he had the hardihood to call upon his counsel to sustain him, by endorsing his statements, that he had expressed a wish to them to plead guilty in order to save Aaron, which was a base fabrication, and afterwards indignantly denied by them.

CHAPTER XVIII.

A FEW hours before the execution of the Longs and Young, John Long informed a friend of Baxter, that when Fox buried the money in the bluff on the Des Moines River, he made certain land marks by which he, or his friends could find the money, as follows:

"At the point where Fox left Birch, to go and bury the money, he made the figures 72, on a large black walnut tree. Seventy-two yards from this tree in a northeast direction is a small black walnut tree with a cross cut in the bark with a bowie knife; fourteen yards from this small tree, due north, is a large stone; midway between the tree and stone is the spot where the money was buried.

Soon after I returned from Fort Madison, I received this information, and immediately started in search of the money. I found the marks corresponding with Long's description; the fallen leaves from the forest trees had covered the ground obliterating every mark where the earth had been removed, but after a close search I found where the robbers had deposited their treasure, and found three American half dollars, and two Spanish quarters, with other marks which proved that the money had been dug up and removed in the night, doubtless under the direction of Fox, after his escape from Johnson, at Indianapolis.

After the trials and conviction of the Longs and Young, and while the execution was yet pending, a special term of the Court was held at Rock Island for the trial of Baxter and the two Reddens.

It would be unnecessary to give the evidence at length in the case of Baxter, being a repetition of facts already stated in Birch's confession, and other witnesses on the trial of the Longs and Young, backed up by his own confession to Gregg and Johnson, after his arrest. In substance as follows:

Confession of John Baxter.—(To Johnson)—"Jo., I want to tell you all about this matter."

"What matter?" said Johnson; who had not mentioned the crime for which he was arrested.

"The murder of Davenport."

"Is it possible that you are guilty, Baxter?" said Johnson.

"Yes," said Baxter, " I am guilty, but I never wanted old man Davenport *killed.* I got into the scrape and could not help it. I became acquainted with Birch, who gave me a description of other members of the gang, when they came up to rob Davenport. John Long came to my house and enquired for me, but I was absent. When I returned, my sister told me that a gentleman had called and enquired for me. I knew from her description that it was John Long. I went out in search of him, and found John and Aaron Long, Fox and Birch, eating their dinner on the Bald Bluff, back of Spencer's, with their pistols and bowies out, lying by them. They said they had come to rob Davenport, and wanted me to do as I agreed, but I desired to have no part in the matter. They told me I never should go home alive if I did not fulfill my promise to them."

"John Long was anxious to rob Davenport that same night, but I told him he would have to kill the whole family. Consequently it was postponed three or four days, until the 4th of July, when I knew there would be a public dinner at Rock Island Town, and thought that Davenport's family would all be there, and that we could then rob the house without hurting any one. I held constant communication with them until the morning of the 4th of July, when I saw Bailey Davenport and asked him 'if all the family were going over to the celebration?' He told me 'they were.'

"I then went up into the woods above James Copp's, where the boys were secreted, and told them the coast was clear, and returned to town. When the news reached town that Davenport was murdered, I ran up the slough to see if the skiff was there. I found that it was, and then I knew the boys were safe. If they had not got away, I was going to tell the whole story, and have them taken up. I want to know if there is any chance to turn States' Evidence? If there is, I want to avail myself of it, and if I get out of this scrape I will live and die an honest man."

This confession with the other evidence doubly confirmed the guilt of Baxter. After the usual arguments of counsel, and a brief charge, the jury retired, and soon returned a verdict of *guilty*, and the Court proceeded to sentence Baxter to be executed on the 18th day of November, 1845.

In the case of Baxter, a writ of Error to the Supreme Court, the judgment reversed and the cause remanded back for a new trial.

The two Reddens were arraigned on an indictment as accessory to the murder of Davenport before the fact. A strong array of evidence was brought to bear against them, but the jury disagreed—eleven for conviction of murder, and one against it, and the prisoners remanded to jail to await another trial, at a subsequent term of Court.

In February, 1846, another special term of Court was held at Rock Island, for the trial of Birch, Baxter and the two Reddens.

Birch obtained a change of venue from Rock Island to Knox County. Baxter also took a change of venue to Warren County. Both cases were continued until the November term, 1846.

In the case of the two Reddens, the prosecution not being able to obtain the witnesses who were present on the former trial, the indictment charging them as accessory before the fact, was dismissed.

Wm. H. Redden plead guilty to an indictment charging him as accessory after the fact, and was sentenced to the State Penitentiary for the period of one year; three weeks of the time in solitary confinement.

Old Grant Redden was released, and made tracks on the Mormon trail for the valley of Salt Lake.

At the November term of the Warren County Court, Hon. Norman H. Purple presiding, John Baxter's case came on for trial.

The same witnesses were brought forward, and the same fact proved, as at the former trial at Rock Island. The case occupied the court during two days, where it was submitted to the jury, who after a short time returned with a verdict of guilty as charged in the indictment.

The sentence of death pronounced by Judge Purple evinced a deep sense of the prisoner's position, and a full and proper sympathy for him. We think it will not be misplaced to give it in full.

"John Baxter! A jury of the country nave found you guilty of murder—the highest and most aggravated offence known to the law. And in your case ingratitude and the ties of friendship severed, and confidence betrayed, have tinged your guilt with a deeper and darker stain. The murdered man had been your friend and patron, you had once been an inmate of his family, and but a short period of time before his melancholy and tragical end, you had enjoyed the hospitality of his house, and under pretence of the partiality and attachment of a friend, had warmed and wound yourself into his confidence and affections.

" The time also which was selected for the consummation of your purposes, marks its commission with more than ordinary turpitude, you had no cause of hatred or even of complaint against the deceased.

" Money seems to have been your only incentive, no inward, long concealed and 'pent up' malignity of heart arising from wrongs and injustice inflicted and often repeated, impelled you to the commission of the deed. But without any other apparent motive than that of gain, on the 4th day of July, a day hallowed and sacred to national devotion and festivity, while a whole race of freemen were rejoicing in, and rendering thanks to Heaven for the blessings of a free government, and the fancied security of their property and persons, under the benign and salutary influence of just laws and 'equal rights,' you and your confederates in crime, invaded the sanctuary of home, and coolly and relentlessly slaughtered an aged and venerable man without compunctions or remorse.

" A just and righteous retribution for blood, thus demands the life of the offender, not alone by way of punishment for the offence, or expiation of the crime, but also as a salutary warning and example to those who may come after. Remember then, that although the law demands your death, that death is no atonement for your crime, nor does it abstract one, either from the overwhelming weight of crime and guilt which rests upon your soul.

" When the penalties of the law shall have consigned you to a premature and untimely death, there is a higher power to which you must answer for this act, as well as for the conduct of your whole life. Let then the space of time allotted you here be spent in deep contrition and repentence. Prepare yourself to die! Your time of life is short, and much remains to be accomplished. Expect not, hope not, for the interference of the executive in your behalf, or that chance or accident may aid you to escape from your impending doom. Such hopes and expectations will be idle and visionary, and will only tend to retard the work of repentance and reform, which is so indispensible to your future eternal state of being.

" Your life is forfeited to the laws of your country, and you must die a disgraceful and ignominious death! It was not in the power of an impartial jury, or able and zealous counsel, who have stood up most manfully in your defence, it was not in the power of the court to avert the sentence of the law and save you from your impending fate. To Heaven alone you must address your prayers for mercy and forgiveness—as you must die, die penitent and like a Christian—and though the forgiveness of the world cannot restore you to life, and the endearments of society and friends, yet the tear of sympathy will sometimes be shed over your early and ignoble doom—and those who have known you here may not wholly curse your memory.

"Black and unmittigating as your crime may be, however much you may have scoffed and derided the laws of God and man, you may, if sincerely penitent and humble, still hope for pardon and salvation, through the renovating power and stainless purity of the REDEEMER'S BLOOD. To that beneficient power and mercy, with the deepest emotions of pity and compassion, I commend you to your eternal destiny.

"The sentence of the law, and the sentence of the court is, that you be taken from this place to the jail of the County of Warren, from thence to the place of execution, and that on Wednesday, the ninth day of December next, between the hours of one and four o'clock P. M. of said day, you be there hanged by the neck until you are dead, and may God Almighty save your soul."

The next week after the trial and condemnation of Baxter, Birch's case came on, in Knox County. He made affidavit for a continuance until the June term, 1847, sustained by a further affidavit by his attorney, Onslow Peters, Esq., of Peoria, Illinois. The continuance was granted. I had an interview with the Sheriff of Knox County, in whose custody Birch was held, and gave him an outline of the desperate character of the man in his charge, assuring him that the utmost vigilence was requisite to keep him safe until the next term of the court.

Through the exertions of his counsel, Lieut. Governor J. B. Wells, Baxter obtained a writ of Error to the Supreme Court, which after hearing the arguments of counsel upon the several assignments of error, confirmed the judgment of the court below.

Baxter's attorney, his other friends and relatives, however, procured from the Legislature of Illinois, a commuta·

tion of his sentence, to that of imprisonment in the Penitentiary for life, where he is now confined.

Birch remained in jail at Knoxville, Illinois, until the 22d of March, 1847, when he broke jail, made his escape and is yet at large.

Thus terminated the trials and disposition of the ten members of the Banditti, that were arrested for the murder of Miller, Liecy, and Col. Davenport.

15

CHAPTER XIX.

IT is due to the public, to my friends, ana to yourself, that the facts relative to the conspiracy formed against me through the influence of Haight, supported by the false testimony of members of the Banditti, should be briefly stated.

As soon as the several indictments at Fort Madison were procured, a desperate effort was made to give publicity to my arrest, accompanied by all the base slanders and falsehoods which the gang were capable of inventing.

Many of the public journals of the day gave admission into their columns of articles against me of the most slanderous nature. After the several trials were over, at the fall term of the Rock Island Circuit Court, and I had slightly recovered from the effects of a six month's cruise against the Banditti, which was crowned with unparalleled success, I had prepared myself to attempt the re-capture of Fox. The gang aware, or suspecting my intentions, made one more effort to destroy me, and save their friends.

The fall terms of court having closed in the several counties the only Grand Jury in session was at the United States Circuit Court for the District of Illinois, held at Springfield, The gang, therefore, headed by the same notorious Haight, brought their efforts to bear at that point.

Upon the testimony of A. B. Williams, sustained by others of the gang, a bill was found against me in December, 1845, charging me with counterfeiting the current coin of the United States.

At this time I was on my way to Springfield, intending to proceed from thence south, in pursuit of Fox. At Rushville I met with the Hon. T. J. Tnrner, on his return from Springfield, who informed me that the gang had succeed in getting me indicted, at that place; and had also succeeded to some extent in prejudicing public opinion against me—advising me not to go to Springfield under the present excitement. I determined, however, to turn neither to the right nor left to shun the villains, but to go to Springfield and meet them on their own ground.

Upon expressing my decision to that effect, Mr. Turner voluntarily tendered his valuable services in my behalf, agreeing to accompany me and render me such legal or other assistance as I might desire.

On arriving at Springfield, I called upon Governor Ford, who being anxious for the re-capture of Fox, advised me to leave at once in his pursuit, and let the present indictments lie for further consideration. This advice with due deference to his Excellency, I declined; fearing that it might be construed into an intention to avoid the process.

I therefore requested the Governor to give me an introduction to the United States Marshal, who, in discharge of his official duty, forthwith took me into custody.

My next effort was to get a continuance, give bail, and leave in pursuit of Fox. Gov. Ford, Mr. Turner, and Mr. Calhoun, Clerk of the Sagamon Circuit Court, voluntarily offered their names as bail.

I learned, however, that the villains had succeeded by their falsehoods and perjury, in arousing a powerful prejudice against me in the public mind. Among other things, I was charged by them of having sworn away the lives of innocent men, (the Longs and Young,) and they alleged that the community of Rock Island had become so indignant against me, that I had been driven from the country and dared not return.

Justice to myself, therefore, required me to remain in custody, and send a messenger to Rock Island to procure evidence of the true statements of the people of that county, who were familiar with my whole course, and the origin of the charges brought against me.

Mr. Turner voluntarily performed the journey, two hundred and forty miles, free of charge.

Had I not already swollen this volume beyond what I anticipated, it would give me unfeigned pleasure to publish the letters received by me, on the returns of mail after Mr. Turner's arrival at Rock Island. They were filled, not only with offers of money and names by the dozen, but there was also a warm hearted, generous, whole-souled feeling displayed in the communications of Dr. Gregg and Mr. Joseph Knox, which touched me deeply. The dungeon grew light, and its dark walls seemed to expand almost to the beauty and brightness of a palace as I read them. Let me here publicly record my thanks to them, not the less sincerely that I feel it was no more than my due.

Mr. Turner returned to Springfield on the evening of the 8th of January, 1846, with a penal bond in the sum of two thousand dollars, signed by a round dozen of the best citizens of Rock Island, which he hastened to file in the District Clerk's office. He thence repaired to the jail where he found me stretched at full length upon a floor of solid timber, wrapped in sweet repose. Truly, a clear conscience can make a bed of thorns " as soft as downy pillows are."

I accompanied Mr. Turner from the jail to the American Hotel, where we partook of a sumptuous repast, there being a great ball in commemoration of the battle of New Orleans.

What a contrast? There the dark and dreary dungeon, where nought but the harsh grating of the iron door as it turns slowly upon its hinges greets the ear of the inmates, as time wears slowly away, each day seeming a little eternity.

Here all the talent, wit, and beauty mingling together, in high glee—the eye dazzled with the display of diamonds and jewels that ornamented the rich apparel of the wealthy and fashionable—and time flies swiftly away, as the gay revellers tripped happily through the intricate mazes of the dance, to the soft wooing of the lute and harp; and as the dawn began to appear, tinging the Eastern horizon with the clear light of a bright winter's morning, the music died away upon the wrapped ear of the listener, and the company separated.

I could fully appreciate the contrast! having been in close confinement from the 25th of December—two weeks.

The following day I addressed a letter to my friends at Rock Island, in which I endeavored to express my full sense of gratitude to them.

While I was detained at Springfield the gang was fully apprised of my intention to go in pursuit of Fox, of which they doubtless informed him. I determined, however, to make a tour in pursuit of him, notwithstanding it was the

express wish of my friends at Rock Island that I should
abandon the pursuit and return home. This would look a
little too much like backing out, and as I considered Fox the
most expert and daring of the gang then at large, I was
peculiarly anxious to have him arrested.

I accordingly started for Indianapolis and Centreville,
reaching the latter place, my old field of operations, in four
days from Springfield.

Sheriff Gentry informed me that nothing had been heard
from Fox since his escape, but that it was the general
opinion of the people that he was lurking in the neighborhood of his father's.

From Centreville I proceeded to Ohio, and after diligent
search ascertained that Fox had crossed the Ohio River and
gone South. I felt compelled, much to my regret, to
abandon the track of Fox, and return to Rock Island.

On my return to Rock Island, I was shown a letter to
Judge Brown, who presided at the trials of the murderers,
the language of which is to profane to give to the public.
But as it portrays the character and depraved morals of the
desperado, and from one of the leaders of the " Banditti of
the Prairies," and being desirous of giving to the reader a
true sketch, I give it verbatim, leaving the reader to judge
of the character of its author and his friends, the Longs and
Young:

" To the Honorable Judge:

" If I should use the word honor in connection with a
name that is as black in the eyes of the world as the d——l
himself. You d——d old stack of carron. I find in looking over the news, that you have passed sentence on two
innocent men, Aaron Loi.g and Granville Young: and J

cannot say that *John Long* was guilty of the crime for which he was hung. True, he was in the crew who killed Davenport; yet, *he* did not kill him. I am the man *who* shot Davenport, and beware, sir! since things have gone as they have. I'll be d——d if *you*, don't share the same fate of the Colonel. The pistol that closed the scene with him, will have the honoi of conveying a bullet through your infernal, old, empty skull. *You* cut a figure on a judge's seat. *Just take that seat again*, and I may be d——d if it won't be the last seat *you* ever take. I carry a six-barrel revolver next my heart, and I carry her henceforth for your *special benefit*—together with the h—l bound jury. You may inform the gentlemen, for well I know them; and if their blood don't atone for the execution of my friends—the Longs and Young—may I be d——d. So, lookout; for, by the time this letter reaches you, I will be close behind.

"I am commander of a company which will, for one blast from my bugle, be at my side; they are true to their cause, and never pull a trigger but what she counts. And this man, *Bonney*, will come up missing when least expected. I knew where the chap was on the *29th of October; he knew it best to be absent on that day; and well the pup knows me, that *intimately*, too. You can inform him that he will see me again, and *only* once more; then I am inclined to think his eye-sight will fail forever.

" And now to the citizens of Rock Island:

' Your rights can never be protected while such a judge is permitted to sit upon the bench; but I shall soon put you to the trouble of selecting another one."

---

*Note.—29th of October was the day the Longs and Young were executed.

This letter was post-marked at Columbia, Adair County, Kentucky, which corresponded with the last track I had of Fox, and was undoubtedly intended to be taken as from Fox, although it was not in his hand-writing.

Birch identified it as the production of Hiram Long, a son of Old Mother Long, whom I met with in the forest near the old woman's residence; doubtless he and Fox were traveling together at the time.

The object of the letter seems to have been to intimidate the court and citizens of Rock Island, and thus favor the prisoners, Birch, Baxter, and the two Reddens, who were yet in jail at that place, and to back up the scaffold statements of John Long. There is a doubt, however, from the evidence and all the circumstances connected with the case that John Long was the person who shot Davenport. If more evidence was necessary to prove that Aaron Long and Granville Young were members of the regularly organized Banditti, this letter itself would be sufficient. As for John Long, he had openly boasted of being a robber by profession, stating that he had broken through and escaped from eleven different jails, and had never before been brought before a court for trial.

As may be supposed, this letter excited only feelings of contempt, and no one was cowardly or weak-minded enough to attach any importance to its threats or statements.

My return to Rock Island in the month of February, 1846, was the closing campaign against the Banditti of the Prairies, and now prepared to meet their false charges, and defend myself against the five indictments pending against me.

In the month of April, the Lee County District Court came on. Although my health was such that it was hardly safe for me to leave my house, I took the steamboat from Rock Island to Fort Madison, for the purpose of meeting the charges brought against me in the four indictments at that place. No witnesses, however, were present at the term of the court, to sustain the charges. The gang were too well aware of the feeling of the people, and dared not come forward.

The prosecuting attorney continued the cases until the October term, on the assurance from Haight that he would then have plenty of witnesses to support the allegations against me. I could not help myself, and was forced to submit to a continuance, and give the villains six months longer to endeavor to prejudice public opinion against me, and manufacture evidence to sustain their false charges.

A severe illness followed my return to Rock Island, and I was unable to meet my accusers at the June term of the United States Circuit Court, at Springfield, Illinois. Consequently the case was continued until the December term, 1846.

In October, I again attended court at Fort Madison. The gang having discovered that their schemes were well understood by the community, dared not attempt to bring forward witnesses, and the several cases were abandoned, and the indictments by order of court dismissed.

One indictment was still pending against me, at Springfield. I learned that the gang were making a desperate effort. My time for several months was occupied in traveling through the country, gathering here and there an item, relative to the movements of the gang in the case pending; to enable me to meet and successfully defend myself against them; not knowing who their witnesses were, or what they would swear, I had no other alternative than to con-

demn them out of their own mouths. Among other items
Haight stated at St. Louis, that he would send me to *Hell,*
or the *Gallows,* if swearing would do it; that he had good
backers, and a little money would buy all the evidence he
wanted. This and other like threats were constantly thrown
out by members of the gang and their friends.

The case came on for trial on the 29th day of December
1846. The gang rallied in considerable force, ready to
swear to anything their leaders might require of them, and
determined at all events to swear me into the State prison,
as their last and only hope of revenge.

The prosecution was conducted by the Hon. D. L. Gregg,
United States District Attorney, assisted by a Mr. Kinney
of Iowa. The attorneys for the defence were Messrs.
Logan and Lambern of Springfield, Joseph Knox, Esq., of
Rock Island, and Judge J. B. Thomas, of Chicago.

The charge of making counterfeit money was fully
sworn to by Dr. A. B. Williams, (upon whose testimony
the bill had been found by the grand jury,) and in part sustained by the notorious Haight, and some others of the
gang from Iowa.

The jury, however, were so well satisfied that it was a
conspiracy got up against me by Haight and Williams, and
sustained by downright perjury, that ten of them wished to
discharge me without leaving their seats. The two others
desired some instructions from the court before rendering
their verdict.

But two of my counsel made speeches in defence, Messrs.
Knox and Logan. They literally flayed Haight and Williams alive. If they failed to satisfy those two individuals
that they were confessed perjured, black-hearted villains,

tney certainly proved it most conclusively to the jury and audience.

The trial took a wide range. The murder of Col. Davenport, the execution of the Longs and Young, and the ways and means used by myself to detect the villains were all laid before the jury. It was well that all this was admitted, for it gave a true history of matters for which the people of Rock Island had been much slandered. I do not think there was a dozen persons present at the court, who were not fully convinced that Haight and Williams sought my destruction, because I had been instrumental in bringing to justice their confederates in crime.

I was certainly most ably defended. No man should attempt to commit perjury, if such lawyers as Logan, Lauburn, Knox and Thomas are to follow on his trail—they are second to no lawyers in the State.

A good deal of anxiety was manifested to hear Knox. He had never before spoken at Springfield as a lawyer. He made a very able and elegant speech. He knew and felt that he was defending a man innocent of the crime for the commission of which he stood charged. Further than that, he felt that to a certain extent he was defending the people of his own country, (Rock Island,) from the slander which had been heaped upon them.

The moment of my acquittal from the charge, and entire freedom from the trammels which the gang had tried to throw around me, was entirely a pleasant one. I had never doubted the result, but I had been worn out and vexed by my long continued struggle with them, and was glad to be at peace once more.

Ten of the jurors signed an address to the Hon. R. J. Walker, Secretary of Treasury, respectfully stating that the facts developed in the trial proved that Haight, who was said to be a confidential agent of the treasury department, was unworthy of such employment, both on account of his *inefficiency,* unfaithfulness and dishonesty.

The address specified various instances of criminal practice, and Governor Ford appended his certificate in support of the charges.

At the request of many friends I give here a copy, verbatim, of the communication referred to with the annexed certificate of Gov. Ford, hoping it will prove interesting to the readers of this brief narrative.

To the Hon. R. J. Walker:

Secretary of the Treasury—Sir:

The undersigned jurors sworn and empannelled for the trial of Edward Bonney, at the present term of the U. S. Circuit Court, for the District of Illinois, on an indictment against him for counterfeiting, deem it our imperative duty respectfully to state that facts were developed during the progress of said trial, riveting conviction on our minds that one Silas Haight, examined before us as a witness on said trial, and said to be a confidential agent of the treasury department for the detection and punishment of counterfeiters, is unworthy of such employment.

Impelled by this conviction, we, therefore, charge that the said Haight is an unfit depository of the confidence of the government, in the important matters confided to his control and management:

1st. Because of his inefficiency.

2nd. Because of his unfaithfulness and dishonesty.

And in support of the first charge, it appeared from the showing of the said Haight, himself, on oath, that he has

never, as yet, in this section of our country since his appointment, been instrumental in bringing any offender
against the laws of the country to justice, although frequently in possession of the requisite proof for doing so:

1st. In the case of one Caldwell in St. Louis, and State
of Missouri; Haight swore that he knew him to be a notorious counterfeiter, and at one time while he (Haight) was
in the employment of the Government, obtained through
the hands of him (the said Caldwell) possession of $25,000
or $30,000 of counterfeit money in St. Louis, but took no
steps for his arrest or punishment, with this evidence of his
guilt upon him.

2nd. It further appeared to our satisfaction, that the said
Haight has long known of the guilt of one A. B. Williams.
hereinafter particularly named, in the matter of counterfeiting, but suffered him to go unpunished and unprosecuted
for a long time; and when the said Williams was at length
indicted, had the prosecutions against him unlawfully and
dishonestly dismissed.

In support of our second charge we say that we are
satisfied that the said Haight has used the power confided
to him by the Government, more for the purpose of defeating than of effecting the ends of justice; that the circumstances connected with the only prosecutions ever set on
foot by him, the time of their commencement, the manner
of conducting them, and the disposition made of them, all
tend to show that such was the fact.

1st. It appears from Haight's own statements that no
steps were ever taken by him for the prosecution of Bonney
on the charge of counterfeiting, until after he (Bonney) had
been actively and successfully engaged in ferreting out
crime, and bringing its perpetrators to deserved punish-

ment, and when his services in that respect were still im-
peratively needed. That when indictments were first found
against said Bonney, at the instance of said Haight, the
Hodges (two Mormon Elders) had been detected, convicted
and hanged at Burlington, Iowa, through the exertions of
said Bonney, for the murder of the German family in Lee
County, Iowa; and that when said indictments were found,
the murderers of Col. Davenport of Rock Island, Illinois,
having been tracked and apprehended by the exertions of
the said Bonney, and three of them tried and convicted;
three of the others were awaiting their trial at Rock Island,
while one of them who had been arrested had escaped and
was at large.

2nd. That the said Haight had frequent interviews with
the said murderers in prison, and afterwards John Long,
one of the said murderers, denounced the said Bonney as
guilty of the murder for which the Hodges suffered death,
as above stated, and of counterfeiting, and referred to A. B.
Williams, heretofore named, as a person by whom such
charges against the said Bonney could be proved.

3d. That at the October term, 1845, of the District Court
of Lee County, Iowa Territory, the said Haight did procure four several bills of indictment, to be found in said
court, against the said Bonney; one for the same murder
for which the Hodges had been punished, as hereinbefore
stated, and the residue for counterfeiting.

4th. That for the purpose of procuring the finding of
said indictments, the said Haight had one Hickman, a notorious scoundrel and refugee from justice, taken clandestinely
and secretly before the Grand Jury, and brought back
again into the State of Illinois, when there were writs in

the hands of the Sheriff of said County of Lee for the arrest of said Hickman on criminal charges.

5th. That when the said indictments were found, the said Haight directed the Sheriff of the said County of Lee to take the writs to be issued on them, proceed at once to Rock Island County, in the State of Illinois, (the residence of said Bonney,) and arrest him on them. And one of said indictments being for an offence not bailable by law, to imprison him on it in the cells of the dungeon.

6th. That said Bonney voluntarily surrendered himself into the custody of said Sheriff on said charges, at the same time requesting that a special term of court for their trial might be held, and this not being done, the said Bonney being out on bail afterwards attended at two regular terms of said court, for trial on said indictments, when they were at length dismissed for want of evidence to sustain the charges in said indictments.

7th. That while the aforesaid indictments were still pending, the said Bonney had taken steps, through the assistance of the Governor of this State, to arrest the second time the notorious Fox, the guiltiest of the blood-stained murderers of Col. Davenport, the said Haight procured one other indictment to be found against the said Bonney, in the U. S Circuit Court, and him to be arrested and thrown into prison at this place, thus effectually preventing the prosecution of the laudable intentions of said Bonney.

8th. That the main agent used by the said Haight in getting up said last mentioned indictment, was the A. B. Williams to whom reference has hereinbefore been made, and than whom, in our estimation, a greater villain, in proportion to his capacity, goes not unhung.

9th. That the terms on which the said Haight procured the co-operation of the said Williams in the finding and prosecuting of said last mentioned indictment was, that the indictments pending in Iowa against the said Williams for counterfeiting should be dismissed, and that the said Haight would use his influence to save said Williams from prosecution or punishment thereon.

10th. That said prosecutions against the said Williams accordingly were dismissed, and the said Williams, after having repeatedly said and sworn that he knew nothing against the said Bonney as to counterfeiting, once in the presence of the said Haight did appear before the Grand Jury and afterwards before the undersigned petit jurors, for the trial of said indictment against said Bonney, (as hereinbefore stated,) and testified that he knew the said Bonney to be guilty of the crime of counterfeiting as charged in said indictment, and he was the *only* witness who so testified.

11th. That said Williams, as appears by his own statements, has been long accessory to the making and circulating of counterfeit money, and guilty of secreting a press, made and used for the purpose of counterfeiting, in his own house, at Nauvoo; and of harboring and associating with thieves and counterfeiters, and aiding them by false statements to escape from the grasp of justice; while from the evidence of others, we were satisfied of the said Williams' commission of the most heinous crimes, perjury and counterfeiting among others, and that so far as any moral restraint is concerned, he would not halt in the commission of any crime.

12th. That in our estimation, the said Haight cannot have been ignorant of either the character or crimes of the said Williams, and yet, has not only never brought him to justice, but, on the other hand, as already shown, has aided him in evading and escaping its just demands upon him.

Vouching for the truth of the foregoing statements, and fully impressed with the correctness of the charges based upon them, we therefore respectfully recommend the removal of the said Silas Haight from the position of confidential agent of the Treasury Department, if his services in that capacity have not already been dispensed with

We are, very respectfully,

Your ob't. servants,

WM. PRENTIS,	GEO. W. CLINKENBEARD,
S. F. MCCRILLIS,	C. FRANCIS,
ROBERT M. PATTERSON,	JOHN VAN HORN,
S. P. SHOPE,	ROBERT WORTHEN,
J. M. WARREN,	MICHAEL KENNEDY.

GOVERNOR FORD'S CERTIFICATE.

I, THOMAS FORD, late Governor of Illinois, do certify that I was present during the whole trial of Edward Bonney for counterfeiting, at the December term, 1846, of the U. S. Circuit Court, for the District of Illinois, and heard all the evidence, and I fully concur in the truth of the above statements of the jurors in the case. And I was fully persuaded from the evidence adduced, that the prosecution was put on foot, so far as Haight and the other witnesses against Bonney were concerned, to be revenged on him for ferreting out and bringing to punishment the murderers of Col. Davenport. And for the further object of stopping Bonney from pursuing the residue of said murderers, then and yet at large. THOMAS FORD

JAN. 6th, 1847.
16

CONCLUDING REMARKS.

I have at length brought my narrative to a close. My principal reason in giving it to the world will be evident to all—that is, to place before the public a true statement of matters which have been much misrepresented and misunderstood. Any defence of myself which may appear in these pages, I am proud to say was not needed among the community in which I reside. By them, my conduct has always been understood, and my motives fully appreciated, but in other portions of the States of the Northwest, this simple narrative of facts may seem to enlighten error, and disarm prejudice. I commend the book to the attention of the reading community, not for any brilliancy in style, or beauty in sentiment, but simply as a record of true events, occurring in our own day, and in our own midst. I have not sought to make myself the hero of a story, and I claim no credit for my successful crusade against the band of robbers and murderers, except that of having done my duty to community. In looking back over the transactions connected with the pursuit and capture of these men, I can recall no one act which I regret, for I believe that circumstances justified the deceit which I adopted to accomplish their detection. Moralists and enthusiasts may plant themselves upon the position that deceit is never justifiable. In the spirit of a lower but far more practical philosophy, I can only point to the result, and venture to assert my own belief that the end justifies the means. I felt compelled to meet the gang with their own weapons, and had I followed the stern tenets of a high morality, the scaffold and jail would have been without their just appendages. " Verily!

the children of the world are wiser in their day and generation than the children of light."

So far as my narrative alludes to life in the West, I
believe that it presents true and faithful pictures, confined it
is true, generally, to a class of the community whose characters develope only the worst aspect of human nature.
Such delineations, however, cannot but have their interest
even to the fair and gentle reader who may chance to peruse
these pages—a fearful and abhorrent interest it is true, but
no less absorbing than the fanciful crimes which fill the
pages of poetry and romance, adorned though they may be
by the master skill of genius.

Could I have drawn upon the imagination it would have
given me pleasure to consign to their just punishment *all*
the base and cowardly murderers of the venerable Davenport. Although the man who did the deed perished on the
scaffold, the master spirit, he who planned and controlled
and guided in the whole transaction, escaped through the
basest treachery and villainy. Yet who shall say that the
pangs of remorse, and the fearful shadows of his darkened
life forever clustering around his heart, the ghost of his
murdered victim rising before him, when he lies down to
sleep and when he awakes, may not be inflicting upon him
a continual punishment, more fearful to bear than the darkness of the dungeon, or the terrors of the scaffold? His
end is sure! Sooner or later his sun will set in blood.
Under other names, and in remote regions of our country,
Fox and Birch are doubtless still pursuing their career of
crime; but the arm of the law or the vengeance of heaven
will overtake them at last.

I would, also, if I had brought imagination to my aid,
have endeavored to add more interest to my several charac-

ters, by embellishing them with some fancied attributes, which would have made their villainy more splendid and attractive; one should have had the graceful rascality of a Paul Clifford, another the daring address of a Robert Macue, and another the deadly brutality of a Black Beard. I would have endeavored to have thrown the charm of some manly qualities around my precious rascals, but as it is, I give you " a plain, unvarnished tale"—a record of unmittigated vice, and cowardly crime.

The result of the trial and punishment of the murderers of Davenport, has been to completely rout and disperse the gang from the North and Western part of the State of Illinois, and from Iowa, their former theatre of operations, to which I trust they will never return.

And now, reader, gentle or ungentle, farewell! We shall never meet again upon the literary field. This is my first and last book. It is not without its moral; I pray you, find it.

THE END.